Every Day A Holiday

"*Elizabeth Ellis's words jump off the page* and into the secret part of your heart where you keep treasured memories and sacred feelings. She sings to you of her life and the lives of others with whom she intersects. Compassionate and thought provoking, an Appalachian/Texan with a whole-world point of view with a little rabble rousing thrown in, Elizabeth Ellis is a true master of the written and spoken word."—Robin Bady, Storyteller, Arts Educator, Brooklyn, New York

"*Elizabeth Ellis is a storyteller who touches her audience* in such a deep, caring way that you can almost hear them sigh, let out a deep breath and think to themselves, 'she knows.' We have all waited for a long time for these wonderful stories of the human spirit and its triumph to be published and the wait is over thanks to Parkhurst Brothers." —Dan Keding, Circle of Excellence storyteller and author, Urbana, Illinois

"*In the forty-some-years* of the American storytelling revival, Elizabeth Ellis has been one of our most treasured truth tellers. Here she tells her own truths—some full of hope and others hard to hear. But in the hearing or the reading of these narratives, we are called to resilience, generosity, wisdom and love." —Milbre Burch, storyteller and workshop leader, Columbia, MO

Every Day A Holiday

A storyteller's memoir

Elizabeth Ellis

Parkhurst Brothers Publishers

MARION, MICHIGAN

www.parkhurstbrothers.com

Parkhurst Brothers books are distributed to the trade through the Chicago Distribution Center, and may be ordered through Ingram Book Company, Baker & Taylor, Follett Library Resources and other book industry wholesalers. To order from Chicago Distribution Center, phone 1-800-621-2736 or fax to 800-621-8476. Copies of this and other Parkhurst Brothers Inc., Publishers titles are available to organizations and corporations for purchase in quantity by contacting Special Sales Department at our home office location, listed on our web site. Manuscript submission guidelines for this publishing company are available at our web site.

Printed in the United States of America

First Edition, 2014

2014 2015 2016 2017 2018   16 15 14 13 12 11 10 9 8
7 6 5 4 3 2 1

Library of Congress Cataloging-in-Publication Data

Ellis, Elizabeth, 1943- author.
  Every day a holiday : a storyteller's memoir / Elizabeth Ellis. -- First edition.
      pages cm
  ISBN 978-1-62491-039-5 (alk. paper) -- ISBN 978-1-62491-040-1 (alk. paper) -- ISBN 978-1-62491-041-8 (ebook)
  1. Ellis, Elizabeth, 1943- 2. Storytellers--United States--Biography. 3. Storytelling. 4. Narration (Rhetoric) I. Title.
  GR55.E56E45 2014
  398.092--dc23
  [B]
                          2014016157
This book is printed on archival-quality paper that meets requirements of the American National Standard for Information Sciences, Permanence of Paper, Printed Library Materials, ANSI Z39.48-1984.

Cover and page design: Linda Parkhurst
Cover Photography by: Paul Porter
Acquired for Parkhurst Brothers Publishers
    And edited by: Ted Parkhurst

102014

For
Scooter
Reo
Christopher
Ruby
and
Jeff

ACKNOWLEDGEMENTS

Thanks to my family for being the source of a never-ending supply of great stories. Continual embarrassment to you, but pure joy to me.

Gratitude to those who have given me opportunities I never dreamed of: Ted Parkhurst, Joseph Sobol, Delanna Reed, Gail Rosen, Robin Bady, Meg Gilman, Kate Dudding, Jane Stenson, Jo Tyler, Ellouise Schottler, Jerry Falek, Gini Cunningham, Michael Baefsky, Dina Stansbury, Elizabeth Jannasch, Ellen Shapiro, Motoko, Laura Packer and Kevin Brooks.

Thanks for making me look good: Paul Porter, Scooter Ollis and Linda Parkhurst.

Honor to Allen Damron, David Ruthstrom and Tim Tingle from whom I learned so much.

To the folks at the International Storytelling Center, especially Susan O'Connor, and the Timpanogos Storytelling Festival for their continued faith in me.

Admiration to Karin Hensley and Kit Rogers and the Board of N.S.N. for all the work done in support of storytellers everywhere.

To the whole crew of Tejas tellers who allowed me to work alongside them all these years. I only have this one page, so fill in your own name right here._____
_____.

For expecting the best from me: Toni Rhegness, Gene and Peggy Helmick-Richardson, Connie Pottle.

Appreciation to all those whose support has made the difference: Dr. Orvel Crowder, Ann Elizabeth Bishop, Cathy Crowley, Gene Edgerton, David Claunch, Marjorie Schaefer, Libby Tipton, Brooks Myers, Nancy Kay Gabbard, Rayanna Talley, Dan Keding, Loren Niemi and Gayle Ross.

Contents

OLD CHRISTMAS
Thirteen Days of Christmas

Driving toward my house I saw the sidewalks were decorated with used Christmas trees piled out for the garbage man. My small granddaughter noticed them too. In an accusatory voice, she said, "Christmas is over."

"Not at my house" I answered.

She dug in her heels at that and said, "My Grandmother says Christmas is over."

"There is still a lot of Christmas left at my house."

"My Grandmother says that Christmas is over and anybody who doesn't know that is crazy."

"Well, at my house Christmas is so important that it lasts for twelve days. Which do you think is better? One day for Christmas or twelve of them?"

Her whole face changed. "Twelve is better!" We passed a few more orphaned Christmas trees. "Why does Christmas last longer at your house?"

"People have celebrated the Twelve Days of Christmas for a long time. There is even a song about it. I'll play it for you when we get home."

"Sing it for me now."

And so I started, "On the first day of Christmas my true love gave to me a partridge in a pear tree."

"Oh," she said, "I know that song." And so with much drama on the part about five golden rings, we sang that old, old song the rest of the way home.

As the years went by there was no more discussion of when Christmas should be celebrated or how long it should last. Her Granny did it differently than her Grandmother. That was true for lots of things. I guess Ruby got used to it. Christmas was one of those things.

Our big family Christmas celebration was planned for Twelfth Night, Old Christmas Eve. The tree was up, the candles were lit. The whole house smelled of scrumptious. And that was even before I put the gingerbread in to bake.

"Want to help me make the gingerbread?" Silly question. She might be nearly a teenager, but some things had not changed.

"I want to lick the bowl," she grinned.

I took a small box from the windowsill. "Are those the fortune telling tokens?" she asked.

"Yep. We'll bake them in the batter the way we always do."

"I wanna put them in."

"Okay, but make sure they are completely covered with batter. We don't want anyone to see them and cheat on what their fortune will be."

She gave me a strange look. "Nobody would do that."

"I don't know," I said. "Didn't your Dad take two pieces last year to try to make sure he got the coin so he'd make a lot of money during the year?"

"I think he just said that so no one would say he couldn't have two pieces."

"Maybe you're right," I said adjusting the temperature on the oven.

After dinner I said, "I hope you all saved room for gingerbread." There was a general round of "I couldn't hold another bite." But it was accompanied by the clatter of stacking plates to make room for dessert. I cleared a load of dirty plates to the kitchen and brought the gingerbread back, setting it in the middle of the table.

"You got this recipe from your Mother, didn't you?" my daughter Reo asked.

"Yes, she used to tell me that it came originally from Rebecca Boone."

"Who was Rebecca Boone?" my son in law Jeff asked innocently. My son and daughter both turned to stare at him. He shrugged, "Sounded like a reasonable question to me."

Reo asked him, "Where did my grandmother live?"

"In Kentucky."

"Yeah, but where in Kentucky?" she persisted.

"Booneville ... oh, I get it. Daniel Boone. Rebecca must have been his wife, right?"

"On the nose, " I said and the room fell quiet since we don't usually talk without mouths full.

"Here's the ring in my piece," said Peggy. Some friends are really family at Christmas.

"That stands for romance, right?" asked Ruby.

"Sure does," said Peggy, and turning to her husband Gene she added, "Don't forget ... Romance!"

Gene grinned and said, "I'll see what I can do."

"Here's the dime," chimed in Ruby. "I'm gonna get a lot of money this year."

Jeff said, " I got the nail. I know it stands for travel. I understand the ring for romance and the dime for wealth, but I never have gotten how the nail would stand for travel."

" It's supposed to be a horse shoe nail to stand for travel. But I lost it soon after moving here to Texas. I keep meaning to get a horse shoe nail but I never think of it until it's time to put the tokens in the cake."

Reo said, "Well, that regular nail must be working because Jeff and I are planning a trip to England and Scotland this year in honor of our twenty fifth anniversary."

There was a general round of good wishes and much "have you two really been together that long?"

I noticed my friend Gene pushed his chair back and left the room.

Reo held up the thimble. "Sorry you're going to be working hard this year," said her brother Scooter in mock sympathy.

"It could have been worse," she said. "I could have gotten the safety pin." There were hoots and hollers in response to that. No one at the table wanted the token that predicted a baby.

"That's all the tokens. No need to take such small bites now," Scooter said.

"No, better keep at it, "I said. "I added an extra token this year."

Just then Scooter pulled a small key out of his mouth. "What's this supposed to stand for?"

"Knowledge or wisdom," I answered. "I found that key this year and decided I'd add it. It isn't traditional, but why not?"

"Knowing this family, it will be considered tradition when we see it next year."

Everyone laughed when a strange figure appeared in the doorway. She was clothed in a long purple dress with lots of flowers on it. A picture book hat with lots more flowers completed her ensemble. It looked strange with her long flowing beard.

"I'm here to sweep all the troubles out of the house," declared Old Bett. She began the work of sweeping out troubles and anxieties and concerns amid an air of merriment. There were lots of calls to "Sweep the trouble off me!" or "Don't forget me!" And there were lots of suggestions about what other family members would want to be rid of. "Sweep out my car trouble," and, "Sweep out my boss."

Old Bett made a thorough course of the room, sweeping all four corners and the ceiling. She opened the front door and with a flourish, swept all our troubles from the year before out of the house.

Photography by peggy Helmick Richardson

Old Bette sweeps all last years troubles out the door.

As "she" turned back toward my bedroom to change clothes, Scooter whispered, "Thanks, Gene."

After the presents had been passed out, the house began to look like an explosion at a wrapping paper factory. I said, "All of you know that the Twelve Days of Christmas come from the change in the calendar. When they moved from the Julian to the Gregorian."

"Why did they change the calendar?" Ruby asked.

Scooter answered, "The seasons and the calendar were out of sync with one another. They changed the calendar to make them match. To do that they skipped ten days. But the people in England wouldn't use the new calendar because the Pope was in charge of it. And they weren't going to let the Pope tell them what to do. A couple of hundred more years would go by before they began using the new system. By then there were twelve days difference."

"Right," I said. "A lot of people think that Old Christmas is another name for Epiphany because they have been falling on the same day of the last one hundred and twenty years. But one is figured on the lunar calendar and one on the solar calendar. They aren't the same holiday at all. And to make it all come out even, every 120 years we have to add an extra day. This is the year. 2012. Now we add an extra day and there will be Thirteen Days of Christmas."

"You're kidding, "said my grandson Christopher.

"No. I'm not! Thirteen days from here on."

"Does that mean we will have another verse to that song?" asked Jeff.

"As a matter of fact, yes," I said. "I am throwing down a challenge right now. In preparation, I got a little cash together as prize money. Whoever comes up with the best new verse gets the prize."

There was the anticipated round of "How do we decide?" "Who gets to judge?" "Does one person get all the money?" "Are there any rules?" "Can there be a tie?"

So the contestants began to put forth their best entries. Some made no sense at all. Some were starting to get raunchy, as in "Thirteen moons a mooning," with the offer of a demonstration.

Ruby offered, "Thirteen cookies baking." There were nods of approval.

Jeff's "Thirteen coins a clinking" was a general favorite.

But when Scooter updated it with, "Thirteen cards a charging," everyone agreed it was certainly in keeping with what Christmas has become for many people.

So the song was sung from start to finish with lots of fanfare for the part about the "five golden rings" which we got to sing an extra time because of the addition of the new verse. And the general consensus was that being the youngest, Ruby, should get the prize money whether her verse won or not.

And we all trooped into the New Year with full stomachs and light hearts.

My Mama's Gingerbread Recipe

½ cup of melted shortening
½ cup of white sugar
½ cup of molasses
2 cups of flour
½ teaspoon of salt
1 teaspoon of soda
1 teaspoon of ginger
1 teaspoon of cinnamon
1 cup of hot water
– Combine the sugar, salt, shorting and molasses.
– Add the sifted dry ingredients, alternating with the hot water.
– Bake at 350 degrees for 45 minutes or until it springs back when pushed down in the center.
– When I make it, I always double it. That fits nicely in a sheet cake pan. One batch of it wouldn't go very far with my family!

This recipe has been passed down in my family from "somewhere back in the greats". That expression is Appalachian for "I don't know how many generations." My Mama always said that it came to the Gabbard family (my Mama's people) from Rebecca Boone.

Photography by peggy Helmick Richardson

**Old Bette looks like she's trying out for a part in the musical
"South Pacific"**

VALENTINE'S DAY
Meddling At Walmart

I was living under the same roof with my grandson Christopher but I didn't see him very often—he was a teenager. Mostly I would see evidence of his existence: those huge shoes in the middle of the living room floor, the back half of him sticking out of the refrigerator. I remember that I spent a lot of time talking to his bedroom door.

You can imagine how shocked I was one night when he came out of his room and spoke to me face to face.

He said, "G". That's me.

He said, "G, it's gonna be Valentine's Day. I need some flowers. I gotta go to school tomorrow. After school I need to go to calculus tutoring. When calculus tutoring is over I gotta go to play practice. It's gonna be way late when I pull up in the driveway tomorrow evening."

I tried hard not to look interested. I said, "I could get some flowers for you. What kind of flowers do you want?"

And he gave me that look that teenagers give parental units and said, "Duh! I need red roses."

I thought a little bit about what it would be like to be that brainwashed that early in life, but I know that when you deal with a teenager you should pick your battles. That one wasn't even on my radar screen that day.

So I said, "Okay, I can get some for you." I was so busy thinking about who those flowers might be for that I let him get in his room with the door closed before it occurred to me to ask who was going to pay for them. Dang!

The next day the phone was ringing off the hook as it sometimes does at my house. It was nearly noon by the time I got my purse and headed out to my car. By now I knew that red roses at the flower shop down on the corner, Flowers by Lorilee, were probably going for seventy five dollars a dozen. So as I headed down the street my car made a right turn into the Walmart parking lot of its own accord, although I don't drive that kind of car.

I got out and went inside. There was the most beautiful bank of flowers I had ever seen. Every conceivable color, and one bouquet of red ones left. They didn't look so good. They'd been passed over by a lot of people. But, I know that when you are sent for something by a teenager, you should never think for yourself. I scooped them up and placed them in my buggy, thereby establishing ownership.

As I was standing there, I stopped thinking about my teenage grandson and started thinking about my grown up son, the world's most unromantic individual. I was wondering how sick it would be if I bought a bunch of flowers and forced him to give them to his girlfriend, when these two guys came running in. You know these guys. You have waited at your house for these guys. They had their names sewn over the pockets on their shirts. They looked at that amazing variety of flowers and they said, "All the red ones are gone!" One of them said, "I told you we should have sneaked off early this morning and come over here. Now my wife's gonna know I waited till the last minute. I'm a dead man." They looked like deer caught in the headlights.

I said, "You know, you don't have to buy red ones."

They said, "We don't?"

I said, "No. Why don't you look along there till you see a bouquet that reminds you of your wife. Buy those and take them home to her and tell her why you bought them."

One of them said to the other, "We gotta do something and we gotta do it fast 'cause we still have to go over to the card rack and read every one of those cards and get back to work before they miss us."

I said, "You don't have to do that either. Just go over to the card rack and buy the first card you see that says 'To My Wife.' It doesn't make any difference what is printed in it. What matters is what you're going to write inside it. Why don't you take all the time you were going to spend reading all those cards, go out to the truck, and write something in the bottom of the card. Write something from your heart. You know, if you go over to 'Flowers by Lorilee' and spend seventy five dollars on a dozen roses, they're still going to be dead by the weekend. But if you write something from your heart on the bottom of that card, it's likely that it will still be in your wife's lingerie drawer in five years."

They were gone like a shot.

I was standing there wondering what Dr. Phil would have to say to a woman who would buy flowers for her grownup son and force him to give them to his girlfriend, when a man came running in.

He said, "All the red ones are gone!"

I thought, "I could help him."

So I said, "Why don't you tell me something about your wife and I'll help you pick out something real pretty for her."

He said, "My wife is a very unusual woman. She can't stand for anything she has to be like what other people have."

I thought, "And you were gonna buy red roses for that woman!"

He continued, "She has the prettiest pink dress you ever saw. It's been hanging on the back of our closet door for months now. My wife hasn't had it on even once since Mrs. Williams came to church one Sunday in that same dress."

I said, "Look over there. Do you see those lavender roses?"

He said yes.

I said, "Did you ever see lavender roses before?"

"Well, no," he said, "I don't think I ever did."

I said, "That's because they are still fairly rare. Why don't you buy one of those bouquets of lavender roses and take them home to your wife. Tell her you bought them because they are as unique as she is." He was gone like a shot.

I was standing there wondering what color roses my grownup son would prefer to be forced to give to his girlfriend, when another man came running in. He said, "All the red ones are gone!"

I thought, "I'm getting good at this."

I said, "You're not from around here are you?"

He said, "No, how can you tell?"

I said, "By the way you talk. Where are you from?"

He said, "Chicago."

"What brought you all the way down here to Dallas?"

He said, "I fell in love with my wife and she was from Texas. You know how they are, she wouldn't live anywhere else."

I said, "You gave up your home for her."

He said, "I didn't give up anything. Wherever she lives, that's my home."

I said, "If you write that in a card, you're gonna be a

happy man tonight."

"Look over there," I said. "Some of the freshest and most beautiful roses here are the yellow ones. Why don't you buy a bouquet of those and take them home to your wife. Tell her that you choose them because she's your Yellow Rose of Texas."

He was gone like a shot.

"Meddling at WalMart"

I was standing there trying to decide if I had enough money to buy more than one bouquet so that my grownup son could have a choice of colors of flowers to be forced to give to his girlfriend, when another man came running in.

That man never mentioned the color of the roses.

He walked along looking at the different bouquets. He pulled back a petal here and there to see which were the freshest. He lifted some out of the water to examine the stems. Finally he settled on a big bouquet of salmon colored roses.

As he pushed his buggy by me, I said, "Your wife's gonna like those."

He said, "These aren't for my wife. They're for my mother-in-law."

I said, "I've been standing here for a long time. And if you don't mind me saying so, you're the first man I have heard say that he was buying flowers for his mother-in-law today."

He said, "My father-in-law died a few weeks back. I promised him I'd be buying these flowers today."

"I see."

"No you don't," he said. "Do you know the best thing that ever happened to me?"

I said, "No, sir, I can't imagine."

"I was lucky enough to marry that man's daughter when we were still teenagers. We slipped off from school and rode the bus up to Oklahoma. You could get married awful young in Oklahoma back in those days. We only had enough money to stay two nights. Then we came back to

Dallas. We went to her Mama and Daddy's house and told them what we had done. He took me out on the porch, just the two of us. He said, 'I can't stand you. So I'm gonna have to make a man out of you so that I won't have to come back and kill you later on.' I never had much family. Never any that counted for anything anyway. And back in those days if somebody was mean to me, I'd be twice as mean right back to them. That's the way I was raised. He had ever reason to be mean to me, but he wasn't like that. He took me under his wing. He taught me what it means to be a man. Nearly everything I know about being a man, I learned from my father-in-law."

"A few weeks back we went on our fishing trip down to Lake Whitney, like we always do when I take my vacation. While we were down there he had a heart attack. Sitting there on the bank beside him, I was praying that the ambulance was going to come in time. All he cared about was wondering if his wife knew how much he loved her."

He said, "I wrote down word for word what I'm supposed to write in the card." He reached into the pocket of his jacket and pulled out the blue envelope the Dallas water bill comes in. I'd know those envelopes anywhere. I've been writing checks and sticking them in those envelopes for over forty years now. I wanted more than anything in the whole world to ask him to read to me what was written on that envelope, but I didn't have the nerve. Fortunately I was a very unruly child. I can read really well upside down.

By standing on my tiptoes and looking straight down, I could read … but only the first line.

It said, "You have been the greatest blessing of my life." Then he rolled the envelope up and pushed his buggy off in the direction of the card rack.

And I decided I did have enough money so that my grown up son could have a choice of colors of flowers to be forced to give to his girlfriend.

If you could use a storyteller, I would be delighted to come and share my stories with you. But, I can't come on Valentine's Day. Ever since then I spend the entire day at Walmart.

EASTER
I Can See All of Me

I was weary to the bone from a long trip out on the road. It was Good Friday, but my dining room table was elbow deep in receipts and tax forms. I knew how I was going to spend the day. I would be wading through a financial wilderness. The due date for filing my income tax was nipping at my heels.

No time to lose, it needed to be done now.

One of the first receipts my hand fell on was for a movie I had taken my little granddaughter to see. I wasn't so sure but what I had liked it more than she had. The next thing I knew I was dialing the number to her apartment.

I was surprised when my granddaughter answered the phone instead of her mother. I knew that money had been tight at their house lately, so I asked, "Ruby, do you have an Easter basket?"

Her very small voice answered, "Yes, ma'am."

"And do you have eggs and candy for your basket?"

"Yes, ma'am," and then conspiratorially she continued, "but they don't know I know."

I grinned at that. "And do you have a new dress to wear for Easter?"

"I don't think so."

Ruby was little, but she was a girl. I couldn't imagine that she wouldn't know whether or not she had a new dress. I said, "May I speak to your Mother?" When Martha came to the phone I asked, "What is Ruby going to wear for Easter?"

She answered, "You bought her an Easter dress last year. I thought I'd put that on her again this year." I could see a potential problem.

"But, last year she wore a size 4. Doesn't she wear a six now?" It seemed to me that my granddaughter looked a lot like Bambi lately—lots and lots of leg.

"I didn't think about that part," said Martha.

I looked at the piles of paper in front of me and grinned. A valid reason to put off my yearly fiscal archeological dig. "It seems to me that we need to go shopping. What we have here is an Easter dress emergency."

Martha was as delighted with the idea as I was.

When I picked them up I couldn't help noticing that Ruby was dressed as usual in pale pink. Now my granddaughter inherited her mother's tall willowy body, but she has my son's darker coloring. Pale pink makes her look sickly. I wondered if Martha was reluctant to let her grow out of baby pink since she is an only child.

As we all know, there are things you would say to your own flesh and blood that you would be reluctant to say to your daughter-in-law. I admit I sometimes speak to Ruby, hoping that her mother will listen to what I am saying. I am sure a family counselor would have a field day with that idea.

I said to Ruby, "You have to wear uniforms to kindergarten every day."

She said, "Yes, they won't let you go to school unless you dress like a boy."

"Nonsense," said her Mother. "You know very well that you can wear skirts to school."

Ruby looked at me and rolled her eyes, as though wearing a skirt made from the same material as a plumber's uniform had anything to do with dressing like a girl. I continued my thought, "Since you have to wear uniforms to school every day, mostly people pick out your other clothes and buy them for you. You don't often get to choose clothes for yourself. But you are getting to be a big girl now, and today is a day when you get to choose for yourself."

Martha looked at me as if to say, "Do you really think this is a good idea?"

I was persistent. "Since you are going to start choosing your own clothes more, there are some things that might be good to know. You know how there are four seasons of the year?"

She nodded.

"Well, people are divided into four seasons, too. The color of their hair and their skin and eyes show us what colors would look best on them. Look at your mother. See her blonde hair and blue eyes? She's a 'spring.' What looks good on your mother are all the colors of flowers in the springtime: pale pink, light blue, yellow."

Ruby nodded. "Mommy looks pretty in flowers."

I said, "Aunt Reo. She's a 'fall.' What looks good on Aunt Reo are all the colors that leaves turn in the fall. And pumpkins."

"She'd look funny in a pumpkin," said Ruby. I agreed with that.

"Now you, you're a 'winter.' You are Ruby. You are our precious treasure. What looks good on you are all the colors of jewels. Rubies, like your name. But also sapphire blue, emerald green, amethyst, even ivory and ebony. All those are your colors."

I wasn't sure she had understood what I was trying to tell her, but when we got inside the store, her mother pulled a pink dress off the rack and said, "This is pretty."

Ruby stepped around her and pulled out a bright blue one. "Is this a 'winter?'" she asked. I said yes, indeed it was. And Ruby continued to pull out others with vivid jewel colors, while her Mother continued to pull pink ones off the rack.

Before long there was quite a pile of dresses on the buggy. We headed for the dressing room.

I decided to appoint myself the wardrobe mistress.

As I took dresses off the hangers and checked for evil, lurking straight pins, Ruby slipped out of her clothes. I popped the first dress over her head.

"You might like to look at it in the mirror," I told her.

Right outside the cubicle we were using was a three-sided mirror. There was another one behind it on the opposite wall. I guess Ruby's shopping experience had been even more limited than I imagined.

Standing in the middle between the two angled mirrors, her face broke into a magnificent smile.

She said, "I can see all of me! I am beautiful!" I was aware that she said it as a simple statement of fact. "I can see all of me. I am beautiful."

My mind went tumbling back through the years to an Easter when I must have been about the same age that Ruby was now. I stepped quickly into another cubicle because I did not want my granddaughter to see my tears.

A woman gave my mother a piece of fabric. It was butterscotch plaid with a bright blue thread running through it. My mother had a lady in our neighborhood stitch up a little suit for me. It had a box jacket with a little pleated skirt. Because she was the lady that made all the bridesmaids' dresses in our neighborhood, she lined the jacket with a piece of blue satin left over from someone's dress. I thought it was the most beautiful thing I had ever seen.

I was a child long before the day of special church services designed for children. We sat with our parents, and we were expected to be both still and quiet. It was unseasonably warm for a spring day. The fabric of my new suit was hot and sticky in the church. I squirmed and fidgeted. My Mother whispered, "Be still." I tried. But I was miserable.

I said, "Mama, I'm hot."

She whispered, "Take off your jacket and hold it on your lap." I was pleased to do that.

The service dragged on. I sat with the jacket on my lap, looking at the blue satin lining. It was so beautiful. I began to stroke it with my fingers. My Mother whispered, "Stop that." So I did. At least I tried to. The blue was so appealing. The satin felt so good against my skin, before I knew it, I was stroking the lining of the jacket again. My Mother punched me with her elbow. "Stop that." This time her voice sounded angry.

I wasn't sure why it was wrong, but I knew I wasn't supposed to touch the lining of the jacket. That was what was making my Mother angry. So I was really careful not to touch the jacket again.

I was really careful, but nobody told my fingers to be careful. They slipped into the jacket and stroked the lining.

"Stop that!" my Mother hissed. This time she took the jacket and held it on her lap.

When we got home from church, my Mother did

not go to the kitchen the way she always did. This time she went straight to her sewing box. She got out her meanest, sharpest scissors. She sat down and cut the lining out of the jacket.

I stood in front of her with tears rolling down my cheeks. "Why, Mama? Why can't I have it, Mama?"

"Wanting pretty things is wrong. Wanting to be pretty is wrong. Keep your mind on the things of Heaven. I don't want you to grow up and go to Hell. Now take this and throw it in the trash."

I stepped back out of the cubicle. Ruby was still lost in the joy of looking at herself in the three-sided mirror. I said, "Let's try on the next dress." And so one by one, I slipped them over her head. With each she stepped into the hallway to look at herself in the mirrors.

Each time she said, "I can see all of me. I am beautiful."

I know some beautiful women. Even though I ran through the Rolodex inside my mind I was unable to find a single woman I know who could stand in front of a three way mirror and say that. Oh, I know some who might be able to say, "This dress makes me look beautiful." But, the power would be given to the dress. I could not think of a single woman I knew who would really be able to claim that for herself.

I wondered how much of that is stolen from us. And

how much of it we give away.

I wondered what is said to boys to steal their power from them. I though I knew some of those things. "You're too short." "You're a weakling." "You're a sissy."

Ruby finally made her selection. It was a red dress with little white polka dots on it. It had tiny cap sleeves and a big sash that tied in the back. I was surprised at how much it looked like a dress I might have worn when I was Ruby's age. The only new thing—in keeping with contemporary fashion—was that the bottom eight inches or so of the full skirt was made of a different material. It was of solid red material with a kind of satin finish.

When we got out to the car, Martha said she was not feeling well. She climbed into the back seat and lay down. Ruby climbed into the front seat. It was Easter weekend, so getting out of the parking lot was bound to take some time. I looked over at Ruby. Her fingers were stroking the satin finish at the bottom of the dress. I smiled at her. "It feels good, doesn't it?"

"It feels beautiful," she said.

"If you scoot over a little, I can touch it too."

And so I drove us home with just one hand.

MOTHER'S DAY
Mama Wasn't A Traveler

I made the thousand mile trip from my driveway in Dallas, Texas to my Mother's driveway at the head of the holler in Kentucky. When the hugging and the kissing was over, you know where I went.

To the bathroom. You would have, too.

On the way back, I cut through the dining room because it saves time. There, in the middle of the dining room table was a postcard from the Great Wall of China. I thought it was strange that anyone who had been to the Great Wall of China knew my mother at the head of the Kentucky holler. Don't you think that's strange?

Since it was a post card, you know what I did. You would have, too.

It was from my cousin Ginny Ruth. She said that she and the other teachers on this trip were having so much fun that she couldn't imagine that the University of Kentucky was going to give them graduate credit for going to China. And, that when she came home she would come and show us all her pictures.

I took the postcard into the kitchen. There was my Mother in her usual spot, stirring something. My Mother thought that gravy was a beverage.

I stepped up beside her and held the postcard out so that she could look at it. I said, "Mama, Ginny at the Great Wall of China! Don't you think that's wonderful?"

She said, "If you like that kind of thing."

"Mama, if you could go anywhere in the world, and money was no object, where would you go?"

She said, "Upstairs to bed."

Mama was not a traveler! You'd think I would have remembered that because I once tried to take her somewhere. But, I want to go everywhere. I want to go everywhere so badly I kept forgetting that Mama didn't want to go anywhere at all.

I was raised on classical music.

Hank Williams. Bill Monroe. Johnny Cash. Mother Maybelle and the Carter Family.

American classical music, wouldn't you agree?

Every Saturday night when the Grand Ole Opry was over, my Mama would turn off the button on that old fat brown radio, she would turn to me and say, "One day I'm going to go to the Grand Ole Opry."

Years and years later, I was a grown woman with children of my own. I was sitting on the public service desk at the Dallas Public Library. Reading the newspaper, I spotted a story in the travel section that said they were building an amusement park in Nashville, Tennessee. When it was completed, they were going to scoop the Grand Ole Opry up out of the old downtown Ryman Auditorium where it had always been held, and carry it out to the amusement park. They would call that place Opryland, and there the Grand Ole Opry would stay for evermore.

I knew what my Mother had meant when she said she wanted to go to the Grand Ole Opry wasn't some place that had a roller coaster. What she meant was she wanted to go to the old downtown Ryman Auditorium.

I decided right then and right there I was going to take my mother to the Grand Ole Opry before it left the downtown Ryman Auditorium.

This next statement will tell you how long ago this story happened. I wrote away for the tickets! And I soon found out that everybody in America was planning to take their Mama to the Grand Ole Opry before it left the Ryman Auditorium. They said I could have my choice of two dates: I could have July … or July.

There was a problem. A big problem. You might not see right off what the problem would be, so I will help you with that.

I was a children's librarian. Still don't see the problem?

In those days, children started to school, decently

and in good order, when children should start back to school.

Right after Labor Day.

That meant they would get out of school for summer vacation about June the 5th or 6th. It would already be 102 degrees outside. Children would run outside to play. That would last about an hour. Then they would beat it down the street to the first free air-conditioned building.

That's your public library.

And they would stay there all day, every day, all summer long. So if you went to work in a public library in Dallas, and probably any other Texas city, you signed a contract that said you would never, in this lifetime, or any lifetime granted to you in the future, ever ask for a day's vacation in the summer time.

I had signed one of those contracts.

I went to my boss. I told him about that old brown radio. I told him about the Grand Old Opry. I told him about the old downtown Ryman Auditorium.

He said, "No!"

I told him about my Mama. I told him about Johnny Cash. I sang three full verses of 'Wildwood Flower' for that man.

He looked directly over my shoulder at the seven children pulling adult reference books off the shelf and said, "Not just no, but get out of my office."

Now we come to the part of this story you are going to find really hard to believe.

I can be really obnoxious. I knew you weren't going to believe that part.

But it's true.

I set to work, early and late, pestering that man about letting me take Mama to the Grand Old Opry before it left the old downtown Ryman Auditorium.

One day, I got him worn down so far he said, "If you'll tell the rest of the staff you're having surgery, I'll let you go."

I have never told another living soul that he let me have a vacation in the summer time.

I wrote away for the tickets. When they arrived, I wrote my Mother and told her when we would be going. On the right day, I got in my station wagon and started backing down my driveway.

My children wanted to know, "Where are we going?"

I proudly stated, "We are on our way to take Grandma to the Grand Ole Opry." It turned out that wasn't their idea of a good time. They wanted to know why we couldn't wait till there was a roller coaster. They whined without stopping for a thousand miles, I swear it. When we finally reached Kentucky, when the hugging and kissing was over, you know where I went. You would have too. On the way back, I cut through the dining room, but there was nothing interesting there, so I headed on in to the kitchen.

There was Mama in her usual spot, stirring something.

I said, "Mama, are you packed?"

"For what?"

I said, "Why, for our trip. Maybe you didn't realize it, but tomorrow morning early ... well, maybe not early to you ... but real early to me, we are leaving here going to Nashville to the Grand Old Opry."

She said, "You mean really go?"

I said, "Of course, really go."

She said, "We can't do that."

"Why can't we do that?"

She said, "Oh, Elizabeth, Nashville is an enormous place. I went there one time when I was a young woman. It's the biggest place I ever saw. You wouldn't know how to drive in a town that big."

"Mama, I live in Dallas."

She said, "No, it's too big and it's too scary. We can't go. You wouldn't have any idea how to drive in a place that big."

I said, "Mama, I came through Nashville coming here to see you today."

She said, "You didn't get off, did you?"

"No. I didn't, but that was because I didn't have any reason to. I could have if I'd wanted to."

She said, "But you didn't, and that means you don't know what you're talking about, little missy. Ever since that Wilson boy came home from the service and decided to start himself a business, he ran that television cable right up my holler so I get Nashville on my TV set. Every night when I sit down to eat my supper, do you know what I am looking at?"

"No, Mama. What?"

She said, "The Nashville news. And do you know what I am looking at every night while I eat my Jello?"

"No, Mama. What?"

"The Nashville traffic report. I know a whole lot about Nashville you don't know, little missy. I know that in Nashville they have those cloverleaf intersections. You get on one of those things, you'd start going around and around and around. You wouldn't have any idea where to get off. You'd drive around in so many circles that your car would run right out of gas. When it did, we'd have to get out and push it over in the ditch. When we did that, somebody would be bound to jump out of the bushes and knock us in the head and drive off in your car."

I was getting a real bad headache.

I could see the headlines in the next day's newspaper flashing in front of my eyes. I knew that it was quite likely to read, "Deranged Librarian Murders Mother."

I knew no jury of my peers would ever convict me.

Then I realized there would never be a jury of my peers.

They'd never be able to find twelve children's librarians that had been able to get a vacation in the summer time.

When I got up the next morning, I could tell she was really real guilty. She was packing.

A picnic hamper.

She let me take her the eighteen miles to the local

state park. We ate under a beautiful elm tree at a real nice concrete picnic table.

Well, actually, she never sat down.

She stood at the head of the table and kept picking at her food with her fingers and asking me if I thought we'd get home before it got dark.

Mama was not a traveler.

For years, I thought of ways that I could get my revenge.

I tried living fast and loose. I was trying to die before my Mama did. Just think about it. If I had been able to pull that off, that woman would have had to come all the way to Dallas just to bury me.

She let me take her eighteen miles to the local
state park.

So Mama would rather have a stick poked in her eye than go traveling. I wanted you to know that so you could understand what it really meant when she decided to take a trip. You would know right off that it would have to be something that was really important to her, wouldn't you? Something more important than going to the Grand Ole Opry.

When my Father enlisted in the Army at the height of World War II, Mother was supportive because she could tell how important it was to him. However, Nancy was a very private woman. The thought that the Army Censor would read every word of her letters to her husband, and from him back to her made her almost nauseous. Because of the war, an Army Censor read every letter to or from anyone in the service. The kind ones used a big black marker and crossed out what you were not supposed to read. The ones who did not care used the scissors. They cut out the part you weren't supposed to read. With them you lost the precious words that were written on both sides of the paper

Nancy's concerns were upsetting to George. A few nights before he left for the Army, he had something to show her. "I want you to read this letter," he said. "If you read it you will see that on the surface it is about the weather and the crops and the children."

She read the letter. "Okay. But, why on earth did you take the time to write a letter to yourself as if you were me?" She was truly puzzled.

"I wrote it so I could show you how you are going to send me private messages. And how I'm going to send mine to you," he explained. He handed her a piece of shirt cardboard he had written on.

"Count the words," he said. "Write them down on a piece of paper just like it says on the cardboard."

My Mother counted the words out loud and wrote down the ones that would give a secret message.
She looked at her husband with tears in her eyes. "You wrote that I was dear to you. It's hidden in the letter. The Army Censor will never see it." She threw her arms around his neck. Both felt as if a great burden had been lifted from them.

After George left, Nancy wrote to him every day. He wrote back as often as he could. She treasured every little endearment that they managed to slip by the Army Censor.

At first his letters were about boot camp and how bewildering Army life could be. As the months went by, there were still endearments hidden in his letters. There was other information, as well. His location was a secret. Yet, the code he had developed seemed to be telling her where he was. Nancy became certain that George was telling her he was getting ready to ship out to go overseas. She felt a sense of urgency because she was sure he would be leaving soon.

She talked to her father about it. "I'm sure he's in Hattiesburg, Mississippi, Paw. I want to go and see him."

"That doesn't make any sense," he answered. "Why would he be in Mississippi? If he were getting ready to ship out to go to the battlefield, wouldn't he be on the coast somewhere?"

Her Paw was not the only one who was sure she had

misunderstood what George was saying. Nancy didn't let that deter her. On the strength of the code in her husband's letters, and nothing else, she took her three year old boy and her new baby girl who never stopped crying and boarded the train in eastern Kentucky. She was headed for Hattiesburg, Mississippi.

When she reached Hattiesburg, the town was so full of people you could not get a room anywhere for money or blood. So she did what any Presbyterian minister's daughter would do. She walked downtown to the Presbyterian Church and knocked on the door of the pastor's study.

The man who answered the door looked kindly to this exhausted traveler. She said, "My name is Nancy Ellis. My husband is stationed here in the Army. I came from Kentucky so that he could see the children. But I haven't been able to find a room anywhere. My father is a minister back home. I thought maybe you would be able to help me."

"Well, of course," he said. "Come in and rest. Let me see what I can do."

In a few minutes the minister had made arrangements for her to rent a room for the week in the home of the church's organist. The two women liked one another on sight. When Nancy went out to the Army base to try to connect with George, she felt comfortable leaving her children with the organist.

Because she thought it would be easy to find him, for her it was. After that every day when his duties were completed, George would get some hours of leave. He would sit in the porch swing with Nancy. He would throw a ball for his son. He would hold his baby daughter who never stopped crying.

One evening the organist suggested that she keep the children so that the couple could go to the movies. They saw Edna Ferber's "So Big".

The week vanished all too quickly. It was time for Nancy to get on the train and head back for Kentucky with her three year old son and her new baby daughter who never stopped crying.

No, Mama wasn't a traveler, but she would never regret making that trip. It would be the last time she would see her husband. A German tank would take his life in the fall. And it would be the only time he would see his baby daughter who never stopped crying.

MEMORIAL DAY
Friendship Cemetery, Columbus, Mississippi

I was sitting in a booth in a Denny's in Columbus, Mississippi, with my old friend Betsy Bishop. If you are ever out on the road and you get homesick, go to Denny's. They all look like. You can pretend you are anywhere if you are at Denny's. Even the waitresses look alike at Denny's.

Betsy held up a brochure and said, "We've been to every place that's listed on their tourist brochure except for their historic cemetery."And I said, "It seems a shame to leave Columbus, Mississippi without seeing everything on Their brochure. After all, they printed it in color."

In actual fact, I like to go to cemeteries. I think they are peaceful places. I like to walk around and read the markers and think about the lives of the people who are buried there. I like to read the old fashioned names aloud and wonder what ever happened to all the people named Beulah or Wilfred.

When we arrived at the cemetery, we could tell right away that it was old because it was obvious it was built for the dead. We don't do that anymore. These days we build cemeteries for the convenience of the living, not to honor the dead. If one of your loved ones dies and you want to place a marker on the grave, it will have to be planted in the ground for the convenience of the guy who mows the grass.

But this cemetery was created in the days when we really cared about honoring the dead. There was the most amazing array of funeral statuary I had ever seen. Of course there were depictions of Jesus. There were also obelisks and crosses. There were marble draperies and granite couches.

Mostly what I noticed were the angels.

There were angels everywhere.

There were angels sitting and angels kneeling. There were angels praying. There were angels standing, angels dancing, angels flying, angels ascending. There were angels playing the harp, the flute, the drums. Who knew that heaven had a percussion section?

There were cherubim and seraphim falling down before Him.

Betsy said, "You choose an angel to be your angel and I'll choose one to be my angel."

I said okay. We do things like that.

We kept walking further back into the cemetery. After a while Betsy said, "That's my angel."

It was a small angel, kneeling, feeding a lamb. Looked just like Betsy. The angel, not the lamb.

She said, "Which one's your angel?"

I said, "I haven't found mine yet." We kept walking further into the cemetery. I thought by now we must be coming toward the end of the cemetery. We had walked a long way.

Then I spotted her. I had never seen anything like her before.

It was a family plot. Like a lot of family plots in Southern cemeteries, it was surrounded by a low white picket fence. The family name was Teasdale, like the American poet, but not her family. This angel had thrown herself on a grave in her grief. It cut me to my heart. It even looked like her marble shoulders were sobbing. My Mother had only been dead a few months.

I said, "That's my angel."

Betsy said, "Looks just like you."

I raised my head and looked toward the right. I saw that we were nowhere near the end of the cemetery. Stretching before me, row after row, were headstones. These did not look like the ones we had just walked through. There were no angels. Plain and pointed at the top, gleaming white marble, each of these stones was exactly alike.

Even the inscriptions were exactly alike: "Unknown Confederate Soldier. Unknown Confederate Soldier. Unknown Confederate Soldier." Row after row as they disappeared over the brow of the hill.

I looked to the left. There were just as many graves. Stone after stone, every one cut in the traditional domed shape, they seemed to march over the hill in rows of military precision. The inscription on each of them the same. "Unknown Union Dead. Unknown Union Dead. Unknown Union Dead." Until they too disappeared out of sight over the hill. It took my breath away.

Just then the caretaker of the cemetery came tootling up on his little three wheeled cart.

"Did you find the grave you were looking for?" he asked. He seemed certain we were involved in some sort of genealogy project.

We said, "No, we just like to go to cemeteries."

He gave us such a look.

Then he followed my gaze toward the graves before me. "Takes your breath away, doesn't it?"

"Yes," I said. "Where did they come from?"

He replied, "When people think about the bloody battles of the Civil War, they always think first of Gettysburg. They forget about Shiloh. You may be standing in Mississippi, but you are just a few stops down the train line from Shiloh. The men with names were buried at the first stops."

"How many are there?" I asked.

"Fifty five acres," he said. "More men fell at Shiloh in two days than had been killed in all the wars that America had fought at that time put together."

I struggled to take in the idea.

He said, "These days everything has a website. Even Memorial Day has its own website. If you look at it, it will tell you that in 1868 some Northern general decided that there should be a day in honor of the men who died fighting for the Union. It says that was the beginning of Memorial

Day. But that's not the case."

"Before the War was even over the women of Columbus, Mississippi began to decorate the graves of the 'glorious Confederate dead'. No one remembers the name of the woman who looked at the other side of this little road and said, 'But what about those poor boys? Their Mothers are so far away.'

"So the women of Columbus, Mississippi went back to their gardens and cut more flowers. They brought them by the wagon load, all those old-fashioned flowers you don't see much anymore: dahlias and snapdragons and hollyhock. Folks say you could smell the gardenias before you came in sight of the cemetery. Those women didn't stop until they had decorated every grave here. They decorated the graves of the men who might have caused the death of their husbands and fathers and sweethearts and sons. That was really the beginning of Memorial Day here in America, no matter what some fancy Union general did."

He went on, "This is my retirement job. I don't mind telling you it's a lot harder than I thought it was going to be. I'm tired when I head home at night. I can't wait to get home and plop down in my recliner and drink me a beer. I always try to stay awake long enough to watch the news. And I gotta tell you what I see scares me."

"It seems like we can't even talk to one another anymore. It seems like we can't even have a civil conversation with someone who holds a different opinion than we do."

"I watch the news, and the next morning I come out here and look at these graves. I wonder if it could ever come to this again. Could American blood ever be spilled on American soil by other Americans? I tell you, I watch the news and it makes me nervous."

"If it ever comes to that again, all I can hope for is when it's all over, some woman will step forward and say, 'But, what about these poor boys? Their Mothers are so far away.'"

Photography by Ann Elizabeth Bishop

"The Weeping Angel", Friendship Cemetery, Columbus, Mississippi

FATHER'S DAY
Three Things I Know About My Father

I cannot tell you how many workshops I have presented over the years about collecting family stories. The truth is I have lost count. What I can tell you is that in every single one of them I have said, "One of the functions of story in the family is to keep people alive long after their death."

I said that over and over. I don't know why it took me so long to realize how much it applied to my own family. Everything I know about my Father, I only know because someone took the time to tell me a story about him.

Family folklore says that I was sitting in my high chair, rubbing applesauce into my hair when my Mother received the yellow telegram that told her my Father had been killed in World War II. I have strained and strained to try to remember him. There is nothing there. I was just too young.

That doesn't mean I don't know my Father. I know him really well. I know him well because of the stories that people told me about him.

This is the only photograph of me and my father.
I am 2 months old.

One thing I know about my Father, he was an amazing practical joker. No distance was too far and no effort too great if it would make people laugh. When I was younger I would often be visiting in Kentucky. Older men would come up to me in public places and say, "I went to school to your Father."

That's Kentuckian for saying, "George Ellis was my teacher."

Then they would proceed to tell me about their school years, but it would not be long before they would say some version of, "You know, your Dad really loved to pull pranks. It seemed like he would rather do that than eat when he was hungry."

They would be off on a story about the time he took someone's car apart and put it back together on the roof of their house. Or the time the head of the school where my Father worked cut the budget of the academic departments and gave the money to the sports program. There was a big basketball game a few days later against the school's arch rival. The gym was packed. In preparation for the event, my Father had given a laxative to a large Jersey cow. At half time he led the animal across the gym floor, stopping every few steps to let the cow express her sentiments about the budget cuts.

How bad it smelled and how long it took to clean it up was always a matter of individual telling. But, the heart of the story was always the same. It was Revenge, practical joker style.

I have always loved hearing those kinds of stories about him. The truth is, I believe no distance is too far and no effort is too great if it will make for a great joke. I feel his blood coursing through my veins as I am preparing what I believe will turn out to be a great gag. There is never a time when I feel more like my Father's daughter.

One of the things I know about my Father is that he was a man of honor.

While teaching agriculture at the school, my Father borrowed two stallions from a friend. He wanted to breed them to the school's mares, both to increase their holdings and to improve the blood lines. Before the stallions could be returned there was a fire. The barn where they were housed caught flame during the night. Both my Mother and my Father threw on their clothes and ran to do what they could to help save the animals.

My Father ran into the burning barn and got the two borrowed stallions out of their stalls. He pulled them outside and threw their reins to my Mother, yelling for her to tie them to the fence. He ran back into the barn to try to save the mares that belonged to the school.

The wild-eyed stallions were rearing and kicking. Before my Mother could tie them, they jerked away from her and pitched her into the fence. As horses will do, they ran right back into the burning barn, right into the stalls from which they had just been rescued.

My Father succeeded in driving the mares out of the barn. All of them were saved.

The stallions burned to death because the fire had become so widespread by that time going back into the barn was impossible.

Both my Mother and my Father grieved over the death of those beautiful animals. My Father went to the head of the school and asked him to pay for the horses that had burned to death. The head of the school refused. My Father tried to reason with him, saying that the owner had loaned the horses to the school in order to help the school. But, the head of the school said that the loss of the barn was so large that they could not afford to pay the owner for the horses, and besides there was no paperwork that said the school had to be responsible for the horses.

My Father was furious. He felt that whether or not there was any paperwork made no difference in the matter. The right thing to do was obvious. The man should be paid for what he had lost. Since the head of the school refused to be responsible for the loss of the horses, my Father took a second job on nights and weekends. It took him two years to earn the money, but he did not rest until he had paid the owner the fair market value of the horses.

One of the most important things I know about my Father is that he was a man who was not afraid to be friends with his Mother-in-law. I know that because when I was growing up, any time the subject of my Father ever came up, my Grandma, Elizabeth Eversole Gabbard, did not refer to him as "your Father" or "Nancy's husband".

Every time she referred to my Father, he was always, "my friend George".

A few years after my parents were married, there was a fire in my Grandma's childhood home. When news of it reached my Father, he rushed there to view the damage. He found my Grandma already there, walking around in the yard, looking at the remains of her family homeplace and weeping. He went to her and put his arms around her. He comforted her for awhile and then convinced her to let her son drive her back to the house she shared with my Grandpa.

Left alone, George began an inspection of the remains.

The house had been built in that L-shape which was much used in the eighteen hundreds. There was a lot of damage in the wing that contained the kitchen, too much to make it safe to enter. The smell in that area was repugnant to George since his recent experience with fire. He found the wing that held the bedrooms had not been as badly damaged, so he stepped in there. As he looked around his nausea began to subside. He saw that all the wood was one inch thick black walnut that Old Grandpa Eversole had cut and cured there on the homeplace at the end of the Civil War.

An idea began to take shape in George's mind.

He took down the bedroom doors and carried them to his old truck. The closets under the eaves that Kentucky folk call chifforobes had large square doors; he carried them away, too. He took a crowbar and began to pry the baseboards off the walls. They were fourteen inches high, of inch thick black walnut.

My Father had the idea, but not the skill he needed.

He enlisted the help of the Shop teacher at the school. With that man's willing help, he made a chest of drawers for his Mother-in-law. He found that the doors to the rooms had been singed too badly to use. The chifforobe doors, however, had not been damaged. They became the back of the chest of drawers. The top and bottom where made from those chifforobe doors, too. The drawers were formed deep and narrow because they were made from the baseboards and had to conform to the size of the wood that was salvaged. When the piece of furniture was finished, it had two small drawers at the top and four drawers below. Knobs were made from the turned wood.

No ornamentation was added. Instead they gloried in the clean straight lines of the piece that gave it a kind of Shaker look.

Grandma was deeply moved by his kindness. Having such a beautiful piece of furniture made from her birthplace meant a great deal to her. Many times as I was growing up, my Grandma would point to the chest of drawers and say, "My friend George made that for me. One day, when you are a grown up lady I will give it to you and you will take it to your house to remember him by."

And that's exactly what happened. Well, except for the part about me becoming a lady. That part was always a lost cause.

I don't hear from my brother Tom very often, but one day not long ago he called and asked me if I could tell him the battalion, the regiment, the company in which our Father served. I did not know that, and I told him so. After I hung up, though, I kept thinking about it. It occurred to me that I might be able to find a letter he had written to our Mother during the war. If I could locate one, all that information might be in the return address.

I had brought a lot of my Mother's things to my house in Texas after her death. I felt too drained to spend time with them. I had put them in the closet of the spare bedroom and come out and closed the door gently behind me.

Five years had passed. It did not seem that going through those papers now would be painful. I found I had a yearning to do so. I never thought of my Mother as being a sentimental person. There were no letters in her things. She had saved only some formal paperwork from the Army. Underneath it I found a yellow telegram in tatters, folded and refolded until it was almost worn apart. "We regret to inform you … ."

I moved it so my sudden rush of tears would not fall on it. In memory my Mother's care worn face came back to me. I think I saw her more clearly in that moment than I ever had in my life before, in that glimpse of what the loss of him had meant to her.

During the last forty years of her life, our Mother shared her home with her sister Louise. I was still hungry for the feeling of being with my Mother. So I decided to look through the things I brought when Aunt Louise died. In the middle of old newspaper clippings about women working in factories during the war and postcards sent from their brother Mike in the Navy, I found a letter from my Father. In the upper left hand corner of the envelope were the answers to my brother Tom's questions.

It was not a letter to my aunt. Instead, it was a letter to their Father, my Grandpa Gabbard. It was written at an Army post in Alabama while my Father was going through basic training. The envelope was yellowed and fragile looking, but the handwriting was still legible.

I don't know that I ever read anything more eagerly. My Mother was as married to my Father on the day she died, as she was on the day he did. So it made me smile to read, "I have had plenty of time to reflect upon what a fine wife I have."

That well-known sense of humor was there, even in boot camp. "To be sure keeping up with a bunch of young men is tough. But I have the advantage in that I know how to sit down and rest when the opportunity comes. I am too old and stiff to get down into the position that the Army wants for firing my rifle. Finally the Sargent agreed that since I hit the bull's eye, my position didn't matter." The real purpose of the letter comes toward the end. Evidently my Father had not had the chance to talk to his Father-in-law before he left for boot camp. He felt he had something to explain. Why would a man who was too old to be drafted, a married man with two children, leave his government-protected job increasing crop production for the troops in order to enlist?

"Many men tried to convince me that I could do more for my country in seeing that food was produced. But my answer has been that the sacrifice on my part would not be the same. I have a splendid home, the finest in all the world, and I want the privilege of fighting for it and not letting some other man do it for me. I always want to be able to face my boy and tell him to be a man in all things. May God bless all of you and save you harmless. George Ellis"

So my brother got the information he wanted.

And I got the letter.

I would like to be able to tell you that I am a good person. I would like to tell you that I sent the letter to my brother because so much of it is about him. That would be a lie. I made a copy of the letter for my brother. I even spent the money to copy it on a really good copy machine. But, I kept the original.

I have read it many many times since then. I almost think I could recite it to you.

I am always amazed by it. More than sixty-five years after my Father's death I got to read a letter he had written. I was able to see how he shaped his letters, what his handwriting looked like. I got to read how he expressed his thoughts and what he believed was important. That makes it a treasure.

I have thought a lot about it. If my Father had died last year in Iraq or Afghanistan, there would be no letter for his daughter to read sixty-five years after his death. There would be no handwriting to examine. No expression of his inmost thoughts. There might be an email, if someone bothered to print it off and keep it. But there would be no handwriting. And you and I both know that people express themselves differently when they are writing a letter than when they are sending an email. It's just not the same.

Since then I have been urging people to write letters. So I am saying that to you, too. Write a letter. To whom? To those who are important to you. To your parents who sent you to teacher's college or your children whose baby pictures you cherish. A friend who sat with you at the hospital while you waited for the news. To someone who has helped you along the way. To someone you admire. To someone you have forgiven. To someone who has forgiven you.

In these days when the only things that arrive in the mailbox are bills and solicitations, can you imagine what receiving a letter from you might mean to them? Can you imagine how long they might save a letter if you shared your heart with them the way my Father did? I'm just thinking.

Labor Day
Grandmother's Church Window

When I tell people that I grew up in Tennessee and in Kentucky, they usually think that I lived in one of those states and then moved to the other one. The truth is I lived in both those places at the same time. That might be a little confusing to you. Sometimes it was to me, too.

As soon as my Mother realized that her husband would never be coming home from war, she packed me and my older brother up bag and baggage, and moved us to Tennessee to live in the house in which my Father had grown up. We lived next door to his brother and across the street from his sister. We were in the middle of all his aunts and uncles and cousins. They were a part of our everyday lives. It was her way of making sure that we grew up knowing as much about him as we possibly could.

However, every day that school was closed for two days or more in a row, we went "home". "Home" was always her Mother and Father's house in Kentucky. We were there for every major holiday. We spent the entire summer there as well. We always came back to Tennessee on Labor Day. That didn't have much to do with Labor Day itself. It was just that school always started the day after Labor Day, so we needed to get back to Tennessee to start school.

Since my Father died when I was a baby, hearing about his death was a whole lot like hearing that Lincoln had been shot at Ford Theater. It was something you could feel sad about, but it didn't really seem to have a lot to do with me since they were talking about someone I didn't really know.

Of course, my Mother didn't feel that way at all. I do not have enough imagination to be able to understand how grief stricken she must have been.

I don't remember my Father at all, although I have strained and strained to try to do so. I was in the first grade when they had straightened out all that great madness enough to begin bringing bodies home that had first been buried in France.

So although I do not remember my Father, I remember his funeral very well. Don't you think that's strange? I remember that his coffin arrived draped in an American flag. It sat in the living room right in front of the fire place. A soldier in full dress uniform came and stood at the head of the coffin all day in a position I now know is called parade rest, but I had no name for it when I was a child. Every one in the neighborhood came to our house to pay their respects, probably not so much to my Father who had already been dead for five years, but to my Mother whom they saw every day. The house was bulging with food and people.

In the middle of the afternoon, the minister from the church across the street came to call. We were surprised to see him because we didn't go to his church. Any Sunday morning we were in Tennessee, we put on our best bib and tucker, and got in my Mother's old black Chevrolet. We would go putt-putting into town to a church of a different persuasion.

Rev. Edwards went around and got his cake. He sat down and drank some of his coffee. Then he patted the seat beside him and indicated that my Mother should come and sit with him. He said, "I came to call on you today because it is important. You need to bring your children and come to my church. There is still time for each of you to learn the right way of thinking about things. Then you can be baptized in the right manner. And, then you won't got to Hell like your husband has. You know he was only sprinkled."

That was when for the first time all day my Mother started to cry.

And that's when I spit on Rev. Edwards. There is more than one form of baptism.

After I spit on Rev. Edwards he never wanted me around any more. I had never been to his church for a service, but I would go to the church almost every day. In the front of the church there was a large stained glass window. It was a depiction of Jesus with a lamb in his arms and sheep all around his feet. I bet you've seen one a lot like it.

Underneath the window there was a brass plaque that read, "In loving memory of Elizabeth Ellis." I knew that was my Grandmother. She had died long before I was even born. But, we had been sharing a name ever since I came into the world. So I didn't think she would mind if we shared that window. I thought of it as being my window, after all, it had my name on it. I loved to sit in the front pew and watch the light come through that window and think about things I thought were important.

After I spit on Rev. Edwards he never wanted me around any more. Every time he found me in the church he would throw me out. I learned if you lay down in the pew no one would see your head or your feet. You could stay there a long time and no one would know that you were there.

When running me off didn't work, Rev. Edwards took to locking all the doors and windows. I spent a really miserable three weeks, until I discovered the coal chute.

I would go around to the side of the church, pull down the metal door and launch myself. I would land on the pile of coal, dust the soot off myself and go upstairs to look at the window and think about things. Every once in awhile, Rev. Edwards would spot me and throw me out again. He never could figure out how I was getting in to the church.

The summer that I turned twelve we spent the whole summer with my Grandparents in Kentucky. On Labor Day we headed back for Tennessee. It may sound silly to you but I was so eager to see my window that I jumped out of the back seat of my Mother's car before she even brought it to a stop. I went running toward the church. I wanted to be able to say later, "I didn't hear you." I was that eager to see my window.

I went around to the side of the church and pulled down the metal door of the coal chute. With great joy, I launched myself. It only took me a moment to discover that during the summer my body had betrayed me. I had some body parts that I had not had before. An awful realization came over me. I was never going to be able to get into the church this way again.

It only took me another moment to discover how tightly I was stuck.

I was hanging there in the sooty darkness, but I could feel the warmth of the sunshine on my feet. I realized I was wedged in so tightly I wouldn't be able to get out without help. The only help around would likely come from Rev. Edwards. I opened my mouth and began to yell.

After a time I felt a pair of hands take hold of my ankles. I braced myself for the sight of that overly red face and those distended neck veins that I had come to know so well. But, when I was out in the sunshine, blubbering and wiping coal soot, there was a man I'd never seen before.

He said, "What are you doing?" It was such a reasonable question I was sorry I didn't have a reasonable answer. I just went on blubbering.

He took me by the hand and led me around the corner of the church. We went in the kitchen door. It wasn't locked. He sat me down at the table. From the cupboard he produced two water glasses. From the refrigerator he pulled the largest bottle of Welch's grape juice that I had ever seen in my whole life. He poured a big healthy slug of grape juice into each of the glasses.

He turned on the water in the sink. Placing the grape juice bottle underneath the flow of water, he filled the bottle to the exact point it had been before he poured any out. Then he gave the bottle a shake and put it back in the refrigerator.

I thought any one who would do that would like to see my window.

"We could go upstairs," I told him. "We could sit in the front pew and watch the light come through the stained glass window. But we would have to be really, really quiet. If Rev. Edwards finds us he will throw us out of the church."

He gave me a startled look and asked, "Throw you out of the church? Why on earth would the man do a thing like that?"

I explained to him how I had spit on Rev. Edwards when I was a little girl and why. I think he must have gotten choked on his grape juice, because his face turned red. He started making this strangling sound. His shoulders were shaking and he had tears in his eyes. I started pounding him on the back because I was worried Rev. Edwards would hear us.

He said, "We won't need to be quiet at all. Rev. Edwards has gone away. I'm the minister of this church now."

I told him, "If you lay down in the pew, no one will be able to see your head or your feet. You can stay there a long time and no one will know you are there."

He said, "That seems like it would be a handy thing to know."

We took our grape juice and went upstairs. We sat in the front pews, him on one side and me on the other. We watched the light come through the window and make colored patterns on the carpet. Then he held his grape juice up and showed me how the light would come through it and make a pattern on the carpet, a tiny little pattern.

We heard a car pull up in front of the church. He lay down in the pew, so I did too. The double doors at the back of the sanctuary opened and someone called out, "Is anybody here?" We never said a word. When we heard the car drive away, he laughed till the tears ran down his cheeks.

I said, "I have to go home now." I already knew I was in big trouble.

He said, "Come back any time. The church won't be locked. I don't believe in locking churches. Somebody might want to get in. They might want to pray or something."

The next day when the school bus stopped, I didn't go to my house. I went straight to the church. I was already old enough to know that you never knew if grown ups were telling you the truth. I have to tell you I don't know if I have ever been as scared as I was when I put my hand on the church's doorknob. But it turned. I went straight on in, like I belonged there.

I sat in the front pew and watched the light come through the window. I wondered where my new friend was. In the room that had always been Rev. Edwards' study, the light was burning and I could hear the sound of typing. I knew that meant there was a woman in there, and I didn't want to bother anybody.

Every day that week I went straight to the church after school. It seemed to me that I had a lot of things to think about. There had been so many changes in my life during the summer.

By Friday I was getting more curious. I walked over toward the study and peeked around the door frame. The room looked totally different than it had when Rev. Edwards was there. Now there were book cases on all four walls. They were filled with books. There were papers and magazines stacked on chairs and on the floor. In the middle of the room, because there was no place else to put it, was a desk. Sitting at it was my new friend, and he was typing. Fast.

He glanced up when he saw me and said, "There you are. I wondered where you had gotten to. Come in." When he saw the look on my face, he said, "Do you like books?"

I said, "Oh, yes, sir, very much."

"I bet you bring a whole stack of them home from the public library every week," he said.

"No, sir," I answered. "The books in the public library are only there for the kids who live in the city. If you live out here in the county, they won't let you have any of their books.

I've been trying to get a book out of that library since I was six years old. They've never let me have one yet."

"Gosh, that's too bad. Then I bet you take a lot of books home from the school library every week."

"I bring some books home," I said. "I had read all the books in the school library by the time I was at the end of the fourth grade. So if they ever get a new one, they give it to me first."

"Hump," he said. "Well, come in and look around. If you find a book you want to read, you can take it home with you. I trust you to take good care of it." I couldn't believe he would trust me that much since he knew me so little.

I began to look on the shelves. All the books were big and fat. They all had titles that ended in the same letters: o-l-o-g-y. But in the middle of all those o-l-o-g-y-s, I found a thin blue book. I figured it was my best shot.

I carried it up to his desk. "I'd like to take this one, please."

He said, "An excellent choice. A lot of people read Soren Kierkegaard."

I took the book home. It only took me a few minutes to realize that Kierkegaard and I were never going to be friends. I put the book under my pillow and kept it what I hoped would be the right number of days: seven exactly. When I took it back I was trembling that he would ask me what I thought of it.

He didn't. All he asked was, "Are you finished with it?"

Most sincerely I said, "Yes."

"Look over on that wall," he said. "I don't think you looked over there when you were here before."

Following his direction, I began to look on the other wall. There were still more books that ended in o-l-o-g-y, but the letters in front were different. In the middle of all those o-l-o-g-y-s I found a small gray book. Stamped in purple on the front cover was a picture of a chifforobe exactly like the chifforobe I had in my bedroom across the street.

I took it to his desk, "I'd like to take this one, please."

"An excellent choice," he said. "A lot of people read C.S.Lewis."

So I took home *The Lion, the Witch and the Chifforobe.*

When I brought it back the next day, I wasn't at all worried that he would ask me what I thought of it. But he didn't. He only asked, "Are you finished with it?"

Sadly I said, "Yes, sir."

"The one that comes after it is bound to be here somewhere. Keep looking. You'll find it. I just haven't been here long enough to get my books in order. Say, you wouldn't want to come some day and help me do that, would you?"

"Oh, yes, sir," I said. "I'd like that very much."

I spent the entire week in Narnia. When I brought back the last of those books I found *Black Beauty* and then *Treasure Island* and then *The Wind in the Willows* and then *The Collected Fairy Tales of Hans Christian Andersen.* And after that, I forget.

I was slow as a child, I guess. I would hate to have to tell you how old I was before it began to dawn on me that all those books I had taken home over the years had been put there for me to find. I think it was the year I got a divorce and began to see all those books cropping up on his shelves about being a successful single parent that the light finally began to dawn.

It seems to me that this story is over. To honor my old friend I won't ask you want you thought of it. Instead, I'll just ask, "Are you finished with it?" I thought you were.

Dr. Orvel Crowder, Harvard-educated
Theologian. How he got to East
Tennessee to be a part of my childhood
is a great mystery.

ROSH HASHANA
Just Tell It!

It was my old friend Loren Niemi who first told me about Reuven Gold. He told me a story he heard from Reuven. The story was a Jewish teaching story, but I couldn't get it out of my mind. Maybe it would be more accurate to say I couldn't get it out of my heart. In some ways that was strange. I was a full grown woman before I met the first person that I knew was Jewish. There are not many Jews living in Appalachia. In my childhood diversity meant, "Are you a sprinkler or a dunker?"

Back in those days I was storytelling partners with Gayle Ross. A few days after we got back from Minneapolis, Gayle's friend Marcy came to visit her. I knew Marcy had been raised in the Jewish faith and that she was estranged from her family because she had married outside their faith. I don't know why, but I felt led to tell the story to Marcy.

I asked her, "Do you know the story about the boy

who wouldn't study the Torah?"

She said, "No. Why don't you tell it to me?" I didn't need any urging.

I said, "Well, you have to remember that I grew up in the Appalachian Mountains. I know more about washing feet than I know about Judaism. And I learned this story from Loren Niemi who was raised Catholic and studied for the priesthood. But I can't get this story out of my mind."

There was once a boy who would not study the Torah. Finally his parents despaired of him. They took him to the rabbi. The rabbi said, "Leave the boy with me." The parents were afraid for the boy, but they did as the rabbi said.

The old rabbi took the boy into his study. Laying down on the couch, he pulled the boy down until the boy's ear was resting on the old rabbi's chest. Then the old rabbi began to weep. He wept all afternoon. When the sun was going down, he got up and took the boy home. His parents were struck by the change in their son.

Years later, when the boy had become the most noted of Torah scholars, someone asked him why he spent so much time in the study of that holy book. He said, "Because when I was a child someone explained to me what it really meant."

A few days later the phone rang. When I heard Marcy's voice, I said, "Gayle's not here." Marcy said, "I didn't call to talk to Gayle. I wanted to speak to you. I wanted to let you know that today is my Father's birthday.

I did not know how he would respond, but I decided to call him. Before he could start talking, I told him that story. The one you told me the other day. The one about the boy who wouldn't study the Torah. I just wanted you to know that I have been invited to my Father's house for dinner tonight. He is going to meet my husband and my children."

I did not know then that Rosh Hashanah begins what are sometimes called "the days of awe." I didn't know it. But I felt it. I was in a state of awe. I was awed by the power of a story to pass from spiritual tradition to spiritual tradition and continue to have meaning. I was in awe of the power of story to heal. Mostly I was in awe of the Spirit that gave us story. It seemed to me to be proof of how much we are loved.

I was saddened by the death of Reuven Gold, for by then he was more than a legend to me; he had become a friend. I was told that he suffered a heart attack and was in the hospital. He was very weak and his breathing was labored. But whenever someone would come in to his hospital room to check his vitals or to draw blood or any number of other hospital procedures, the worker would come close to his bed. When they did, that big hand would come up and grip them around the upper arm and pull them down till their ear was next to his mouth. With what little breath he had left, he would tell them a story.

Then he would say, "Don't let the story die. Tell it."

I was told they would often respond with, "But I'm

not Jewish." His answer was, "That doesn't matter. Just tell it."

When any storyteller dies, it is as if a library has burned to the ground. As I was grieving, I wrote this poem about Reuven.

Brother to all things,
You were so orthodox a fool
the blood of Chelm and Coyote both
flowed within your veins.
The holy Name of God
burned upon your tongue
and often singed both you
and those who paused to listen.
Trickster to the end,
the last joke yours.
So soon to put on
the cloak of invisibility
and step beyond
our puny human sight.

Reuven had been dead for several years when a gate change in the Saint Louis airport sent me hustling over to the International Terminal to get my flight home to Dallas. There are those who would say that a flight to Texas from the International Terminal is appropriate because Texas is it's own foreign country. And in some ways they would be right.

Walking down the corridor I heard the sound of

singing coming from another hallway.

I asked the attendant working my gate, "What's all that beautiful music?"

She said she wasn't sure and picked up the phone. After a few words, she said to me, "They say that someone has brought the Torah from Jerusalem. People from the local synagogue came to meet it."

The Torah? I knew what the Torah was. I wanted to see the Torah. So I went running in the direction of the music. There was a large group of people coming down the concourse. Students playing guitars. Mothers pushing babies in strollers. Couples walking together. Grandfathers being pushed in wheelchairs. People laughing and singing and dancing. In the middle of the group was a small elderly man. He was carrying a bundle wrapped in cloth. He carried it against his heart. He carried it the way you might carry a baby. I knew that inside that bundle was the Torah.

In the back of my mind I heard Reuven's voice. "Just tell it."

I tried to ignore it.

The voice refused to be silenced. "Just tell it."

"Here?" I asked. "Now?" The voice spoke again as plainly as I have ever heard a voice that was not audible.

"Just tell it."

"But, I'm not Jewish."

"That doesn't matter. Just tell it." So as the procession approached me, I stepped out in front of the rabbi.

"Sir, I want to tell you a story." He looked at me, and in that moment I saw me from his point of view. I realized that he thought I was going to try to save his soul. I wanted so badly to let him know that was not the case.

At that point something came out of my mouth that I was not even aware I knew.

I said, "The Prophet Elijah appears in many forms."

He held up his hand for those behind him to stop. To me he said, "Continue."

There was once a boy who would not study the Torah. His parents despaired of him. They took him to the rabbi. The rabbi said, "Leave the boy with me." His parents were afraid for him, but they did what the rabbi said.

The rabbi took the boy into his study. He lay down on the couch. He pulled the boy down until his head was resting on the old rabbi's chest. Then the old rabbi began to weep. He wept for the rest of the day. When the sun began to go down, the rabbi got up and took the boy back to his parents. They were dumbstruck by the change in the boy.

Years later, when the boy was the most noted of Torah scholars, someone asked him why he had spent so much time in the study of that Holy Book. He said, "When I was a boy, someone explained to me what the Torah really means."

When I finished the story, the rabbi smiled at me and bowed. Then he continued down the concourse. People walking behind him came up to me and asked, "What did you say to the rabbi?" The stragglers behind them stopped to ask me, "What did you say to the rabbi?"

To each of them I said the same thing, "I told him a story."

"Tell it to us!"

"Ask the people who were standing near him. They know it now. They won't let it die."

**Reuven Gold influenced many of the
leading lights of the Storytelling Revival.**

HALLOWEEN
Ghost Story Aftermath

The producer of the festival said, "A lady who owns an art gallery has generously donated space in the loft of her gallery for all the featured storytellers to stay together. It is beautifully restored and I think you will be comfortable there. So, would you rather have a hotel room or stay with the other tellers?"

I didn't even need time to ponder that. "I would like to stay at the gallery with the other tellers." As storytellers we often work at the same events. Mostly that ends up meaning that we get to hear one another on stage, and we got to drive by one another as passengers in golf carts on the way to our next session. "Great to see you. How've you been?" That is often the extent of the communication between us even in a two or three day event for at the end of each evening we are usually headed to host homes that are spread around the area.

I was really pleased that this was going to be different. We were all going to be staying in the same place, a place that sounded really interesting. A restored warehouse. The producer had said it was lovely. What it looked like didn't matter much to me. I was dreaming of having meals with the other storytellers, of sitting up late at night swapping stories. I imagined the jokes we would tell, the rounds of tales about "the gigs from hell" we would tell. We'd sing together. Many tellers have wonderful voices. I don't do it especially well. That doesn't stop me. I love to sing. I could hear what it would be like for us all to join in singing. Some of the tellers would have their guitars. There was bound to be an auto harp player in the mix. I don't play anything but the radio. But I love music so I spent lots of time dreaming about the folk songs we'd sing, the old hymns we'd share.

During the several weeks that went by before the event, I was filled with thoughts of how much delight there would be in staying at this loft together. When I drove to the festival, I went straight to the art gallery to put my things away and get freshened up before the festival began.

It was an old cotton warehouse sitting right beside the train tracks. You could see where the bales had been loaded from the second floor, the loading docks even with the tracks. The gallery owner showed me around the first floor. The old hardwood floors gleamed; the old brick exposed to new life. There were interesting paintings and masks on the walls, and the floor of the gallery was covered with dramatic sculpture made from several different media.

"We rotate the offerings in the gallery every month,"

she said, "except for the Mexican folk art. That's a part of the permanent collection. I lived in Mexico for several years." I thought all of it was intriguing, but frankly I was in a hurry to get squared away and get over to the festival in time for the sound check.

She showed me the stairs to the second floor. "This door is never closed," she said.

"That's probably a good thing. It looks really heavy," I said, examining the old metal sliding door.

"We wanted to keep as much of the original hardware as possible," she said.

And I told her they had done a wonderful job of restoring a beautiful old building. "It's great to see that it's going to have a long life in its new incarnation," I said.

If the downstairs had been lovely, the upstairs was amazing. Near the top of the stairs there was a very chic industrial style kitchen space, perfect for parties. There were lots of glassware and dishes on exposed glass shelves. Exotic rugs defined spaces for resting and conversation. Leather couches rested next to shabby chic armchairs. The owner's lifetime of travel and excellent taste was exhibited in the folk art displayed throughout the space. It looked like a picture out of a fancy magazine.

The things I liked the best were tall mirrored wardrobes. There were several of them on casters. The big open space was divided by them into sleeping spaces offering lots of privacy. She said, "They work really well for us when we have guest lecturers or artists in residence for the gallery. We simply use them to create as many spaces as we have guests."

"I think it's the most amazing space I've ever seen," I said as she showed me one earmarked for me. I put my things in it and scoped out the bathroom to scrape a little road dirt away before going to the festival. "How many of the other tellers have arrived?" I asked.

"Beats me," she said. "You're the only one who took me up on my offer of staying here."

"I'm the only one who's going to be staying here?" I thought it best to hide my disappointment that there would be no late night rounds of tale telling, no singing of "I'll Fly Away."

"Right," she responded. "And it kind of made me mad that I did all the work to get this ready and no one wanted to stay here. So I'm glad you're here. Listen, I've been working on a grant. The deadline is staring me in the face. I hope you don't mind if I get back to it."

"No, of course not. I need to head out, too."

"We had a break in a few nights back," she said, "and we haven't gotten the locks on the front door repaired yet. So when you come back, just park toward the back of the building and come in the garage door. Here's the remote." And she disappeared down the stairs.

I readied myself as quickly as I could and headed out to work. I made the sound check, led a workshop on folktales, ate supper with folks attending the festival and told in the evening concert. It ended around ten o'clock and was followed by a late night ghost story telling.

I like to think of myself as a competent teller of ghost stories, but the truth is I didn't get the "ghouly gene" like some storytellers I know. There are tellers who excel at the telling of ghost stories. There are even tellers who revel in it. There are those who can tell stories that will chill your blood in your veins even if you have heard the story before. Many times.

I was telling in the ghost stories, the middle teller. I thought of myself as the soft creamy filling between two of the most horrifying ghost storytellers I have ever heard. The two of them were in their element. By the time the concert was over, I grabbed my things in a hurry. I headed out to the dark parking lot grateful that I had company.

It was really late, long after midnight as I began driving back over to the art gallery. On the way I noticed things that I had not paid attention to in the afternoon. The gallery was in a neighborhood that had seen better days. Some folks had put their backs and their dollars into restoration projects, but that was spotty. There were people loitering on the streets. The night air was filled with the smell of barbeque and the low growl of electric guitars. The beer joints and honky tonks were still doing a brisk business. There were people hanging out on the sidewalks in front of each of these establishments. As I drove further into the neighborhood streetlights were farther apart. There were people in vacant lots huddled around oil drum fires, their voices loud and intimidating. The smell of Friday's paycheck spent on food and rough fun was replaced by the smell of garbage. Figures were swaying down the sidewalk in the darkness. I saw one dark figure lying in a doorway. I thought it must be someone who had started celebrating the evening earlier than any of the others. Then I remembered the dead body lying on the ground in one of the stories I had just heard. That body had gotten up and sought revenge. It gave me the creeps to recall it.

I pulled up in the parking lot of the gallery. The building that had looked so hopeful in the daylight seemed skeletal in the dark. I didn't see any lights coming from the building at all. I parked my car right under the overhead light attached to the back corner of the building and looked around apprehensively before opening the car door. I gave myself a shake and said, "Stop being a baby."

I got out of the car and walked toward the alley. Right in front of me, below the overhead light I saw a puddle of blood. Well, maybe puddle is too big a word. But it was blood. There was a lot of it. Someone had stepped in it and the print of it was on the footprints that disappeared down the alley. Down the alley where I had to go to get into the building. I flattened myself against the wall. Having the brick at my back was reassuring. It was a technique learned in childhood. No boogey man could get me from behind. That made it easier to face what might be in front of me. I peered around the edge of the building. Nothing but blackness.

Photography by Paul Porter

"Under the light was a pool of blood. someone had
stepped in it and the foot prints went down the alley
where I needed to go."

I started edging my way down the murky alley an inch or two at a time, the rough brick reassuring against my shoulder blades. My heart was beating so loudly I could hear it in my own ears, like a sound track for the story of "The Tell Tale Heart." That thought made it even creepier. I remembered the one man show I had seen of a telling of "The Tell Tale Heart" and how Christmas carols had been used to help tell the narrative. I thought of how the sound of the telltale heart had been "The Carol of the Bells." It had been the ghastliest thing I ever heard and now I couldn't get it out of my head.

It seemed to take me days to cover the thirty feet down that alley, my head whipping back and forth in search of danger. I finally reached the garage door and pushed the button. For a long and panicked moment nothing happened. Then a groaning noise was followed by the agonizingly slow lifting of the door. As soon as it had lifted far enough for me to squeeze under it, I was inside and pushing the button to send it back down again.

I was safe inside the building. I stood still and took a couple of deep breaths. There was a small blue exit light over a door. I thought perhaps it led to the main gallery. I walked toward it and managed to open the door. I wondered why I had asked how old the building was and how long it had taken to restore it. Why hadn't I asked something practical like, "Where are the light switches?"

The gallery that had seemed so full of life and creativity felt macabre now. The darkness was so thick, I could feel it as much as see it. The sculptures loomed up out of the darkness in alarming angles that seemed to move to cut me off from the door. The faint light showed enough of the masks on the walls to highlight their distorted mouths and evil eyes. It seemed to me that every monster story I ever told had come to life.

I have never been one to give in to faintheartedness willingly. The choices were go back to the car which meant going back into that alley, or go toward the masks. Walking toward the wall, I felt the ragged brick beneath my fingers as I crept my way forward searching for the door to the upstairs. I felt the frames of the pictures and an occasional sharp nail sticking out. I stepped around the dreadful masks that protruded from the wall. But I was sure I was making progress toward the door that led to the stairs.

My hand touched the cold, thick metal of the sliding door. Just a few more feet forward and I would find the opening that led to the stairway. I felt the metal of the door for several more feet forward. Then I felt the brick wall on the other side. I didn't feel any opening. I couldn't have missed it. The gallery owner said it was never closed. I felt my way back to the other end of the door. There was no opening.

I tried to remember the placement of the door from the afternoon. It seemed to me that it had been to the right of the opening to the stairway. So I felt my way along the door again. This time I was looking for latch or lever that would open the door. I had to find it. Going back into that alley to get to my car seemed unthinkable. My search for the latch became increasingly more frantic.

"I've got a gun!" It was a woman's voice, harsh and loud.

I froze in my tracks.

"I'm calling the police."

The police? My frozen brain began to function again. I knew that voice. It was the voice of the gallery owner.

"It's me!" I yelled. "It's Elizabeth. It's your storyteller."

The door began to slide back. The terrified face of the gallery owner appeared in the darkness.

"What are you doing down here?" she said.

"I was trying to find the doorway to the stairs. You said it was never closed."

"Are you just now coming in?" she asked.

"Yes," I said. "The ghost stories just ended a few

minutes ago."

"Oh," she said. "I thought you were already in your bed asleep. I worked on the grant till it got really late and I was sleepy. I have to come into the office really early and finish it tomorrow morning. I thought it didn't make any sense to drive all the way out to the suburbs that late at night just to get up and come back tomorrow. So I decided to come upstairs and sleep. I figured somebody ought to sleep in all those beds I fixed for the storytellers. Since I thought we were both already upstairs I closed the door in case someone broke into the building. I thought you were a burglar."

My heart rate was beginning to diminish. My breath was no longer coming in short ragged gasps. As we climbed the stairs I said, "Have you always carried a gun? Or did you get one after the recent break in?"

"Gun? ... Oh," she said, "I don't really have a gun. Storytellers aren't the only ones who stretch the truth."

THANKSGIVING
And So Jack Goes To Seek His Fortune

Never had a child that I raised actually left home before. Both my son and daughter had rolled out of the nest and down the road to take up residence not so far away in the Dallas Metroplex. The furthest anyone I had raised had ever gone away from home to live was the Dallas suburbs. But now my grandson Christopher, who had gone to college in the Metroplex, was offered a wonderful graduate assistantship at the University of Tennessee.

That meant he would be moving far away from home. And from me.

We sat down and discussed it before he left. "You did the right thing to accept the offer that the University of Tennessee offered you." I said. "No school in Texas offered such a lucrative deal."

"Yes. And they have a great program there. But even with their great deal, money is gonna be tight."

"That's one of the things I wanted to talk to you about. You know that I will help you if you have any emergencies." He nodded. "But money is tight for me right now, too. It's a thousand miles each way from here to Knoxville."

"Nine hundred each way," Chris corrected. "I looked it up on the computer."

"Okay," I said. "Nine hundred. It's a thousand to my Mama's house in Kentucky. I was just going by that. Whether it's a two thousand mile round trip or an eighteen hundred mile round trip, the cost of gas is through the roof. I've never seen it this high. I don't think we can afford two trips back home this year. You can come for Thanksgiving or for Christmas. I wish it were different, but you'll have to choose. I don't see any way we can afford both."

Of course, since the choice was between Thanksgiving and Christmas, Christmas won out hands down.

So in August when he left for Knoxville, I was left behind, knowing that he would not be coming home until mid-December.

For him it was a great adventure. Not so much for me. I found it harder to deal with than he did. He loaded all his belongings into a huge rental truck. He attached a flatbed trailer to haul his car behind it. With the supreme confidence of a young man just in to his twenties, Christopher was sure that he would have no problems on the trip to Tennessee. The nine hundred miles along

Interstate 40 in something that looked to be nearly as long as an eighteen wheeler didn't phase him.

I tried to be supportive. That included not reminding him that he had never even driven a truck around the block before.

In fact, we had the biggest fight we had had in a long time on the morning he was leaving. What were we fighting about? I had the temerity to suggest that he would want to take the paperwork that went along with the rental of the truck. He was equally convinced that he would not need it in the least.

I snuck out to the truck while he was in the bathroom and stuck the paperwork in the glove compartment. By the time he came out, I was standing on the porch looking innocent.

About five and a half hours later my phone rang. In a small voice Chris said, "Granny, the truck has a flat. What should I do?"

I said, "Open the glove compartment. In it you will find the rental agreement. At the bottom of the page you will see an 800 number. Call that number and they will send someone to take care of the tire. It's their job."

"Oh!" Click.

Are we ever ready for their departure? There were so many things I wondered if I had taught him. There were so many things I would tell him if I could have the time back

again. It had seemed unfair to him to run down the street
behind the truck yelling, "Wait! Wait!" I wondered why we
have so many stories about the hero setting off to seek his
fortune and so few stories of his Mama staying home and
trying to learn to live with that.

So instead of yelling, "Wait!" I went in the house
and wrote a poem.

> And so Jack goes to seek his fortune.
> His Mama stands and waves him out of sight.
> Child of her old age, an unbidden gift,
> She sheds no tear until he moves beyond
> The first bend in his bright road.
> He is a good boy, and knows those things
> That can be taught by telling.
> Nine nines are eighty one. Yes, ma'am.
> And no, sir.
> And where those elbows do not go.
> She has seen to that.
> But does he know the things you cannot tell,
> But only teach by living?
> How forgiveness and gratitude can
> Flow across your heart like water over stone.
> That a dream is always worth the risk.
> And can he learn to love himself enough
> To make a sweet life in that new place.
> A place she cannot go.
> A place he will soon call "home".

Throughout the fall neither of us mentioned Thanksgiving. Christopher regaled me with stories of his classes, his work, his friends. As the holiday grew closer, I brought up the subject. "I wish we could afford for you to come home. I hate to think about you being by yourself so far away."

Photography by Reo Hahn

No matter what his name may be, every Jack goes to seek his fortune.

"Oh, it's gonna be okay," he said. "I'm getting together with my new friends. A bunch of them can't go home for Thanksgiving either. We're gonna cook our own dinner. We're planning an 'Orphan's Thanksgiving'. It'll be great."

It was the first major holiday we had been apart. But I was determined to put a good face on things. I said, "That's great. Let me know if you need any cooking advice."

Three days before Thanksgiving my phone rang. A rather lonely voice said, "Granny, if you sat down at your computer, you could write out how you make deviled eggs. I could go to the store and buy what I'd need to fix them. I could make them and put them in the bottom of my refrigerator. On Thanksgiving morning I could get up and start sneaking them out of the fridge and eating them. And you could call me on the phone and yell, 'Stop that. Those are for dinner.' It would be a lot like being home."

I will go to my grave without ever revealing to anyone how much FedEx will charge you to overnight deviled eggs to Knoxville, Tennessee. Suffice it to say, Christopher could have driven home for that amount of money.

Emergencies of that magnitude are why the credit card was invented.

I figured as long as I was sending the deviled eggs, I might as well send some cookies and some brownies and some banana bread. I followed the rather complicated directions given to me by the sympathetic FedEx employee. They included dry ice and punching holes in the bottom of a styrofoam ice chest with a pencil so the gas could escape. Then he reminded me that the styrofoam ice chest would have to be packed into a cardboard box so it wouldn't get caught and torn apart in their mechanized equipment.

I knew Christopher would be in his office the day before Thanksgiving, so I had the package delivered to that address.

When he called me, he was squealing. "I got my package. I got my package. And I went around and I gave everybody some chocolate chip cookies and some banana bread and some brownies."

"But they're not getting any of my deviled eggs!"

The following was sent as an email for future reference ... and to camouflage the package arrival:

Christopher, add this to your recipe book that I gave you when you left home.

HOW TO MAKE DEVILED EGGS

Get a big pot.
Get out the eggs.
Look at each one to make sure it isn't cracked.
Put 6 of them in the pot.
Cover them with cold water.
Bring them to a boil on the stove.
Let them boil for 10 minutes.
Take them off the stove.
Immediately pour off the hot water.
Pour cold water on them.
Let them sit in the cold water for 15 minutes.
Peel them.

Cut them in half lengthwise.
Put the egg yokes in a bowl.
Put the whites on a plate.
Mush the yokes up with a fork.
Add 1/3 cup of mayonnaise.
Add 2 tablespoons of mustard.
Add ½ teaspoon of vinegar.
Get out the olives.
Chop them really really fine.
Add ¼ cup of the olives.
Eat the rest of what you chopped.
Add garlic salt and pepper to taste.
Mix it all up.
Fill up each of the pieces of egg white.
It's easier if you use two spoons.
Sprinkle paprika on the top of them.

– If you want to make a bigger batch, boil more eggs, but don't forget to increase the ingredients.
– Cooking tip: Sprinkle white things like cheese or bread crumbs on dark food. Sprinkle dark things like paprika on light food. It may not make it taste better, but it will look like you tried hard.

CHRISTMAS
Christmas In the Clouds

Most young people head off to college to a sense of new-found freedom. Not me. I managed to attend a college that was even stricter than my Mother, and that was saying something.

Strict? If it was fun, there was a rule against it. We were not allowed to drink, smoke, or dance. Shorts could be worn in the gymnasium, but we had to wear our raincoats over them until we got there. In addition to all the rules in the student handbook, there were lots of unofficial rules. One of them was an eighteen inch rule. That meant you were expected to keep eighteen inches between his shoulder and yours at all times.

Yes, you read that correctly. And the Dean of Women often carried a yardstick—one of those wooden ones given out for free by hardware stores and lumber yards in hopes you would remember to shop at their place for nails or galvanized buckets the next time you were measuring fabric for that dress you were about to sew.

Strangely enough, that eighteen inch rule was suspended every Saturday night from ten o'clock to eleven, which was curfew. That change only applied in the parlor of the girl's dormitory. During that one hour, a girl could sit on a boy's lap. As long as he had a magazine on his lap. As I remember, Reader's Digest was very popular.

One night at dinner in the dining hall a guy sat down opposite me and began talking. I was amazed that he even knew my name. He was cool. He was a senior, and I was a lowly freshman. We did have one class together, so I figured he was going to ask me if he could borrow my notes. I was good at that.

Imagine my shock when he asked me if I would be his date for Christmas in the Clouds. That was the absolute highlight of the entire winter social season on campus. Every girl wanted desperately to have a date for Christmas in the Clouds. Think of it as a winter formal ... with no dancing.

Remember that eighteen inch rule? There would be couples sitting at tables listening to music. There would be solos and trios and barbershop quartets with names like the Harmonetts and the Eventones. The Madrigal Singers were sure to perform. There might even be a recitation or two. But, there would definitely be no dancing.

I was so excited I floated down the hill to my dormitory. I sat down immediately and wrote my Mother that I had a date for Christmas in the Clouds. I explained that I really had nothing appropriate to wear to such a momentous event. I was sure that she could see that I was going to need a new dress for the occasion. And to make sure that my Mother sent a big fat check for the dress, I was sure to include the information that my date, Jack, was studying to be a minister. I knew my Mother would like that, and besides I thought that would increase the numbers on the check. Maybe from Freshman Math, the word "exponentially" came to mind.

In only a few days I received an envelope from my Mother. I pulled out the letter and unfolded it. There was no check. I shook the envelope. No check fell out. I peered down into the envelope just to be sure. The letter was the only thing in it. I was immediately apprehensive.

I began to read the letter. My Mother wrote, "I am happy that you are having a good time at college. Your young man sounds like a nice boy. I am pleased that he asked you to go with him. I have purchased the material for your new dress and have already started making it. I will send it to you as soon as it is finished." There was more to the letter, but I didn't read it. I didn't have the heart.
A queasy feeling arose in the pit of my stomach. My Mother was a woman of many useful skills. Sewing was not one of them.

In a couple of weeks there was a notice in my mailbox, the kind that means you should come to the window to get your package. I didn't try to take the package to my dorm room. I sat with the box on my lap on the bench right outside the post office. I gathered my courage. I couldn't wait any longer to see what my Mother had sent.

It was worse than I imagined. It was made of red and white checked gingham. The neckline started right under my chin. The hem line allowed the toes of my shoes to show. The leg of mutton sleeves looked as though they were designed for a fullback in full uniform. To add insult to injury, it was trimmed in white eyelet.

My roommate found me staring at it later in the day. She said, "You can't wear that to Christmas in the Clouds!"

I said, "I know. I guess I will just have to tell Jack that I have changed my mind and I won't be able to go with him."

"Are you crazy?" she asked. "He is cool. You are going to Christmas in the Clouds. You just won't be wearing that."

She walked toward her closet. "I brought two formals to college with me."

In truth, I already knew that. One day as I was walking past her closet I noticed some white tulle sticking out between the door frame and the door. Of course I did not want any of her clothes to be damaged by being shut up in the closet door, so I had needed to open the door wider to push the tulle safely back into her space. I wasn't being nosy. I was just trying to be helpful. Honest. But, I had needed to take both formals out of her closet in order to move the remaining clothes around to make enough room for the beautiful formals. I wasn't being nosy, only helpful.

She began pulling both dresses out of the back of her closet. One was white with a satin bodice. It had little silver leaves embroidered all over it. The ball gown skirt of white tulle had an overskirt of white satin with the same silver leaf pattern. It was a lovely dress.

The other. Oh, the other. It was dark emerald green. The velvet bodice was attached to an A-line skirt of emerald green grosgrain.

It was dramatic. It was sophisticated. It was strapless!

She said, "I wore both of them to dances in high school. Pick whichever you want. I'll wear the other one. It really doesn't matter to me." Angel child sent straight from Heaven. Until that moment I had never noticed the wings growing from my roommate's shoulders. I wondered how she folded them so that she could get through the door to our room.

I said, "I would die to wear the green one." And I gave her a bear hug when she said okay.

Suellen had come to school with two formals. She had only come with one strapless bra. I had a problem. I set out immediately trying to earn the money for the needed undergarment. I took care of the Dean of Women's incontinent dachshund for an entire week while she was gone to a conference. I babysat for the longest weekend of my life for the Head of the Math Department's twin ten year old boys who were known to other sitters as Attila the Hun and Vladimir the Impaler.

When I figured I had enough money, I caught the bus into town. I went to the best department store and rode the elevator up as the elevator operator called the floors.

"Third floor—Ladies Ready to Wear. Lingerie to the right." She said it right out loud. In front of God and everybody. The women of my family had undergarments. They had unmentionables. They did not have lingerie. Lingerie was a word that wasn't even in my family's vocabulary.

A middle-aged woman came up and asked if she could help me.

Very quietly I said, "I need a strapless bra."

She said, "What?"

A tiny bit louder I repeated, "I need a strapless bra."

In a voice that could been heard clearly over a stadium of screaming football fans, she called out, "Gladys, this girl needs a strapless bra." I was sure there were cheerleaders who would want to take lessons in voice projection from this woman.

A lady with a tape measure around her neck bustled up to me. "You will need a fitting."

I thought, "I don't know you that well." But it didn't matter. She swept me into a dressing room and began disrobing me before I could protest. It was really unnerving. As is often the case when we feel like we might die of embarrassment, I didn't. Soon I was dressed and leaving with a small pink shopping bag with the logo of the store printed on it.

I caught the bus headed back toward school. Since the bus was really crowded I sat in the back. We were getting pretty close to school when a lady started trying to get out the side door of the bus. She was struggling with a baby stroller, a toddler and a lot of Christmas packages. I jumped up and came forward to help her get everything off the bus. Once I sat the stroller on the ground, I hopped back on board. The bus was nearly empty by now, so since I would be getting off soon I plopped down near the door.

I was in my dorm room before I remembered that pink shopping bag. It was on the back seat of the bus. At least I hoped it still was. I called the bus station immediately. I would call several times over the next few days. No one ever turned in my pink shopping bag.

There wasn't time to earn the money to buy a new strapless bra.

Word of a tragedy of that magnitude sweeps through a girl's dorm with the speed of a freight train. The next day a girl who lived up on the third floor that I barely knew knocked on my door. She said that she had come to school with two strapless bras. She said her Mother believed in sundresses because guys like them.

I told her my Mother disliked them for that very reason.

She said that I could borrow one of her strapless bras. By now I didn't even care if it fit.

On the day of Christmas in the Clouds, I took a long time getting ready. I wanted to look my best in Suellen's dark green dress.

When they called up the stairs that I had a gentleman caller in the parlor, I came down the stairs feeling somewhat like Scarlet O'Hara.

Jack had bought me a corsage. A real corsage. At least I believe it was meant to be a corsage. It looked a lot like what they hung around Man of War's neck when he won the Kentucky Derby. But I thought that spending that much money on flowers must mean that he liked me. I helped him pin it on the bodice of the dress and tossed the rest of it over my shoulder, where it hung down and swayed back and forth when I walked.

He gave me his arm and we walked up the hill to the dining hall. It looked just as magical as a decorating committee with very little money to spend could make it look. In other words, I thought it was magical. White lights and tissue paper had created a transformation.

We were seated together at one of the tables. The dining hall had been upgraded with red tablecloths and centerpieces of holly and ivy and candles.

Jack was seated on my left. We ate a meal a cut above the usual dining hall food. That was followed by students who performed several musical numbers just as I had expected. A senior girl read a poem she had written about going home for Christmas.

Jack asked, "What do you think of the turkey?"

I said, "It's good. What do you think of it?"

"It's not as good as my Mother's, but it's not bad," he said.

During the music he asked, "What's your favorite

Christmas song?"

I said, "All I Want for Christmas Is My Two Front Teeth."

He laughed and said he liked it too. "I bet we don't get to hear that one tonight," he whispered. Every time he spoke to me, I turned my head in his direction to hear what he had said. Things were going so well between us I felt positively giddy.

There is only one thing on earth I am allergic to. Carnations. It doesn't matter what color they are or how many of them there are. They make me sneeze. I began doing that not long into the program. The sneezes became more severe as time passed. At one point, Jack looked at me with concern.

"Are you feeling alright?"

I did my best to smile and told him I was fine. He actually patted my hand. A more intense round of sneezing ensued.

Trying to be witty, I whispered, "A few more sneezes like that and my nose will rival Rudolph's."

I noticed that his gaze had changed. He was no longer looking at my face with concern. Now he was staring at the bodice of my dress with a look of horror on his face.

I followed his gaze to the top of my dress. The under wiring on the borrowed strapless bra had worked its way free and was poking out of the top of the dress bobbing back and forth like a pair of demented bug antenna.

I leaped up and ran out of the dining hall. I ran down the hill and up two flights of stairs. I threw myself on my bed and I started to cry. That's a lie. I had started crying before I left Christmas In the Clouds. I lay there on my bed with hot tears stinging my eyes.

The people who design dormitories seem to be students of Japanese architecture. The walls are always paper thin. On the other side of the wall, I could hear my suite mate Leslie. She didn't have a date for Christmas in the Clouds. She must have been using the privacy of her roommate's absence to practice her part as the Narrator of the Christmas Cantata that was being presented the next day.

I guess she was having trouble with one of her lines because she kept repeating it over and over. There was no way to avoid hearing her.

"And it came to pass ... And it came to pass ... And it came to pass."

I thought, "I would give anything if you would shut up."

But the voice continued, "And it came to pass ... And it came to pass." The emphasis or the volume or the tone might vary, but the words were the same. A never ending stream of repetition.

I thought, "If you don't hush, I'm gonna go over there and throttle you." But she just kept on like she was hunting for the Secret Chord or something.

"And- it- came- to- pass ... AND IT CAME TO

PASS."

After a while the chaos of my thoughts began to still. The words began to take some hold inside my brain. One of the meanings they could have began to dawn on me. I sat up and blew my nose. I looked back toward the door. All the snow that I had tracked in on the hem of Suellen's beautiful green dress was melting and making puddles on the floor.

"And it came to pass."

I got up and took off my borrowed finery. I put on the red and white checked gingham dress my Mother had made for me. I brushed my hair and walked back up to the dining hall. I walked through the tables of Christmas in the Clouds. I sat down next to Jack.

He didn't even mention that I had been gone.

I told you he was cool.

EVERY DAY A HOLIDAY
Some Thoughts

I have been musing about how our lives would be different if we treated each day as though it were a holiday. Does that seem strange to you? Remember, I live in Texas and drive long distances in my car alone. I have a lot of time to think.

I went to the dictionary. It defines "holiday" as "a day on which one is exempt from work."

Well, that's not going to fly. Few of us are going to be able to call our bosses to say that we're exempt from coming to work today. I can imagine what the response to that would likely be.

When I worked as a librarian, we put letters on our time cards. H was for holiday. V stood for vacation. S was for sick day. I once called my boss and asked him to put a U on my time card. He asked me what the U stood for. I told him I was too Ugly to come to work that day. He laughed and asked the real reason I was not coming. I told him it really was U—too ugly to come to work. I had dropped my dentures in the sink that morning and broken them. I was taking them to the dentist for repairs, but in the meantime I was too ugly to be seen by anyone. He laughed a lot, but he put the U on my time card. What the personnel office thought of that I don't know. He never told me. I am sure I couldn't have gotten away with that a second time.

The dictionary did say that the word "holiday" comes from the term "holy day." So I looked up "holy." Just as I figured, it said "sacred." I can work with that. It also said "set apart." I like that. It said "characterized by perfection" and "spiritually pure." No, those weren't really what I meant. Then it said "evoking awe." My, that's appropriate.

What would life be like if we treated each day as if it were holy? I suspect that our lives would be richer and more fulfilling. To think of each day as sacred would mean that we did not take the day for granted. We would appreciate it and respect it as a gift that was given to us. No matter what we are called upon to do this day, the day itself is precious.

Should we begin to think of the day as being "set apart," we might begin to look for what makes it special.

Or maybe we would commit to it being special. I was once at the grocery store when a clerk said to me, "Have a nice day." Before I even thought about how it might sound to her I said, "Oh, I plan to do better than that." Why set the bar that low?

If we thought of this day as "evoking awe," we could revel in the joy of being alive in it. Instead of dragging ourselves through it, we might come to understand that there has never been a day like it before, not in the whole history of the universe. And there will never be another exactly like it either. Days are as individual as snowflakes. Little children seem to understand this instinctively. Totally in touch with the joy of each experience, they give themselves whole heartedly to their lives.

To think of a day as "holy" does not mean a great change of what we do in it. We may still need to go to the bank or bathe the dog. The difference would not be in how the day is spent, but in how we think about it. That's how we make each day a holiday. We do that by approaching each day with the knowledge that it is.

When we know there is a holiday coming up, we look forward to it. We have a sense of eagerness and anticipation. We discard our apathy, shake off the humdrum and get excited. We are expecting something good to happen, something lovely. We feel more alive. More connected to the flow of Life.

But we don't stop with the feeling of anticipation. For a holiday, we begin to make plans. We ask one another, "Where are you going on vacation?" or "Do you have plans for the Holidays yet?"

We give thought to how we will spend the time. We lay plans for what we will be doing and with whom. We don't float along. We actively participate in the creation of something beautiful.

Wouldn't we want to do that with our lives every day? Create something beautiful.

We also emphasize traditions. We look to the past to see what customs have made holidays important to us. Thought for those who have gone before may be part of our consideration. The examination of memories for those things that seem most precious to us from past holidays always takes place.

We give focus to our relationships. Some holidays are centered around family. Christmas and Mother's Day are times when our thoughts go to those related to us by blood. Others are centered around friends. The picnics and fireworks that accompany Fourth of July or parties planned for Halloween come to mind. For years my grandson Christopher attended the opening game of the Texas Rangers with our friend Gene. For them it was a holiday in every sense of the word.

Last weekend my granddaughter Ruby came to visit. There is a barbeque place where she really likes to eat, so I thought on Saturday I would take her there for lunch. I even thought that we might take in a matinee if we could find a movie the two of us would both like. That part is harder than it sounds. Since she is a seventh grader, most kids movies are considered beneath her now. Most adult movies are out of the question. We need to pick and choose.

Late Saturday morning she appeared in the doorway of my room wearing cheetah print pajamas trimmed in hot pink. They even had feet shaped like cats. They were spectacular and I told her so.

She said, "Thanks. I got them for Christmas."

I said, "I thought we might go out to lunch today … ." I did not get as far as telling her my plan to eat at the barbeque place she fancies before she cut in.

"No thanks, " she told me. "Today is Pajama Day. I've been looking forward to it all week."

"Pajama Day?" I said. "Is that a holiday?"

"Yep. It is a day dedicated to not putting your clothes on all day."

"Sounds good to me," I said. "Are there any special things that one does on Pajama Day?"

"The important thing is not to 'do' a lot. It's a day for playing with the cat. He misses me when I'm not here. It's a day for watching birds out the window and daydreaming. It is definitely a day for daydreaming. Oh, board games could be part of Pajama Day, too. And naps." The idea had real appeal I thought. This is a holiday I could support.

"Since you won't be getting dressed, I suppose fast

food is appropriate for Pajama Day."

"No," she said. "Pajama Day is a day for slow food. For making something in the crock pot. Something that doesn't require a lot of chewing."

So I got out the crock pot. Stew sounded delicious, and needed a minimum of mastication.

When she walked away, I thought about the things she had said. Pajama Day was obviously an official holiday. It met all my criteria. She had been looking forward to it all week. With the overly scheduled lives of middle schoolers, I could see the appeal for her. She had made a plan. Special activities were to be a part of the celebration. Most of them were things that she had taken joy from in the past. It was to be shared with family and friends. Friends? Don't forget the cat. Sydney definitely qualifies.

That got me to thinking about creating holidays. Don't jump to the conclusion that creating holidays is weird. People actually do that a lot. They may not think of that when they prepare a Super Bowl Party or plan to get together with their old college roommate each year. But that's what it is alright.

Some created holidays are public. A good example is Kwanzaa, a holiday that was designed by Maulana Karenga. He took the customs of African harvest celebrations and reworked them for the contemporary African-American community. The emphasis was to be helping people reconnect with their heritage which had been denied them.

We live in a culture that worships youth and beauty. Women, especially post-menopausal women, are invisible. There has been no observation to mark a woman's move into the later stage of her life. No custom or sacrament to honor that sacred part of womanhood. As we have aged some of my friends have held Croning Ceremonies for themselves. Calling on their female friends to support them, they have designed celebrations that honor woman's age and woman's wisdom.

Each of these is an example of a created celebration or ceremony that has deep meaning for some. Like Kwanzaa, some developed holidays are for the community, publicly held and publicly advertised. Some, like Croning Ceremonies, are simple and private.

Also, like the examples given, some are annual on-going events. Others happen once to commemorate an event that will not be repeated. Either way, they show our search to create meaning in our lives.

The calendar is filled with invented holidays and commemorations. There's National Pickle Day, and Asparagus Appreciation Day. Many of those are just to try to increase sales. There are also those that are just for fun: National Talk Like a Pirate Day. And those that are therapeutic: National Don't Cry Over Spilt Milk Day. That one is dedicated to forgetting about all the mistakes we've made. I'm in love with that one. Story lovers gather in November to celebrate the brain child of J.G. Pinkerton. Called Tellabration, it is a day set aside for listening to stories. In this world of conflict, there is something special in knowing that people all over the planet are doing that on the same day in the same way you are in the far-flung places where they live.

Why not invent a holiday for yourself? No, I'm not talking about your birthday, but I hope it's a great one. I mean a day that has special significance just for you. Maybe you would want to invite folks you cherish to share it with you. Maybe it would be something so private you would never breathe a word about it to anyone.

When you stop and think about it, one of the most commonly held celebrations is the Pity Party. That sometimes gets a bad rap. People may be embarrassed to be staging one. I think those can be quite therapeutic. If you're going to have one, why not elevate the celebration and use it as the opportunity to really get it out of your system? To throw a proper Pity Party, you should send out invitations. (Although I would have to question whether it is a true Pity Party if you can think of anyone to invite.) You should definitely dress in black. You should serve melted ice cream and fallen cake. Bursted balloons are the symbolic decoration of the day. And if there are party guests, each should be issued a party hat with the top caved in. Throwing yourself into the spirit of the event is bound to help you see your situation differently. If not, at least any friends you invite will know exactly how you feel.

Once someone asked me how I was and I said, "I am bleeding to death from paper cuts." No one big thing had happened to make me feel bad, as is usually the case with a Pity Party. I had, instead, suffered a string of small indignities. Now when I begin to feel myself dealing with emotional blood loss, I choose a date for Paper Cut Day. I spend that day alone, doing the things that please me most. I read poetry or a great novel, eat the foods I like best, and find ways to pamper myself because I know that I am valuable and important. Not because of anything I have done, but because I am.

When I moved to Texas at age twenty five, I knew no one here. When Christmas time came, I sent my children back to Appalachia to spend the holidays with their grandparents as I had promised. Before they left, I drove myself to the point of exhaustion putting together all the usual Christmas fanfare for two preschoolers. After their departure, I wandered around for two weeks with nothing to do but feel sorry for myself during the holidays.

Fortunately when I examined that experience, I made an earth-shattering discovery. I discovered that I am responsible for my own happiness. If there was something that made me unhappy, I had the power to change it. Trust me, it was a discovery. I had had no experience with it up to that point.

I could see that the chances were good I would be repeating a solo Christmas experience many times in the future. I decided I would not try to prepare a Christmas celebration for my children before they went to their grandparents. I'd wait till they returned to host ours. That would give me time to shop and plan for the event while they were away. It would have the extra bonus of giving me something to look forward to during their absence.

Since I knew this was likely to be repeated throughout their childhood, I decided to choose a day that would be our special day for celebrating Christmas and make it a tradition. It would feel more grounded, less like it was the hand me down holiday of a single parent home. I remembered my Grandparents celebrating Old Christmas when I was little. I could taste the boiled custard and gingerbread. I remembered they considered that day to be the end of Christmastide. So I chose to place my family's Christmas celebration on Old Christmas.

I guess there are those who think it is disrespectful to tamper with customs. To me it seems disrespectful to continue a custom that has lost its meaning. When traditions no longer meet our needs, we do well to evaluate them. Making thoughtful changes can infuse old customs with new meaning and vibrancy.

Making a decision about when we would celebrate Christmas had a bigger influence on me than I imagined. Since Christmas is the most rigidly held day of the year, deciding to do it differently had transfer value. That decision made it far easier to look at other elements of my life and decide to make changes that supported our family.

Over the years I have developed new holidays to share with friends and family. On Chick Flick Day, I sneak off to the movies with my friend. It is always more fun if we are supposed to be working. My family and I sometimes go off to celebrate Culture Vulture Day, which involves a trip to the museums.

For years I hosted the You Don't Know Me Very Well Film Festival. Every member of the family would show the film they had seen that year that meant the most to them. It is the way I have seen every slasher film I have ever experienced, and every Schwarzenegger movie I have ever seen. When my children were young adults it was an amazing way to learn more about the world in which they lived and what it meant to them. Once long ago, my daughter brought with her her new boyfriend. When he threw himself down on the carpet prepared to watch the video brought by the three year old with the same respect he would give to those brought by the adults, I fell in love with him on the spot. Good thing my daughter married him, huh?

In one of his songs Bruce Springsteen says, "I'm just tired and bored with myself." Well, I don't give every day a special name. I imagine I could if I set my mind to it. Rather I try to grant each day my full attention. Strive to be fully alive in it. And remember that whenever I feel like that Bruce Springsteen song, the lack is not in Life, but in myself.

"Pluck the day, for it is ripe."
—Horace

Elizabeth Ellis, Storyteller

READING GROUP EXTRAS

ABOUT THE AUTHOR

I grew up in the Appalachian Mountains of Tennessee and Kentucky. Because my Father died in World War Two, my Grandfather was an active force in my life. My Mother moved us to Tennessee to grow up in the house in which my Father had been born. Every day that school was closed for two days in a row, we went "home". That was always the home of my Mother's parents in Kentucky.

I was a child who lived mostly in my own head. I never stopped talking, a great cross for my Mother to bear. Most of my closest friends were imaginary. On one level, that is still true today.

The greatest influence on me as a child was Dr. Orvel Calhoun Crowder, the minister of the church across the street from my house in Tennessee. He introduced me to the world of books and the life of the spirit.

After getting an undergraduate degree in English and History from Milligan College, I received my Masters in Education from East Tennessee State University. I came to Dallas to work for the Dallas Public Library as a Children's Librarian, a position I kept for a decade.

In 1978, my old friend Gayle Ross and I made a trip to the Appalachian Mountains to attend the National Storytelling Festival. We met Jackie Torrance, David Holt, Donald Davis and the Folktellers, along with others who called themselves storytellers. On the way back to Dallas, "We could do that!" became "I will if you will!" We came home to Dallas and began plans to become professional storytellers.

We worked as a duo, as The Twelve Moon Storytellers, for about four years or so. But, making a living large enough to support both families was extremely challenging, so eventually we each began solo careers.

Making my living as a storyteller has been a great honor and a great joy. I have gotten to tell throughout the United States and Canada at festivals and conferences. A few years ago, I was invited to come to New Zealand to share my stories. In the last thirty-two years, I have told to more than a million school children. I have received the John Henry Faulk Award from the Tejas Storytelling Association, the Circle of Excellence Award from the National Storytelling Network and the Oracle Lifetime Achievement Award from the National Storytelling Network. Each of these is a great honor, but the greatest honor is when anyone takes the time to listen.

If there is anything I enjoy more than telling stories, it is teaching other people to tell. I present workshops at conferences, intensives in people's homes, as well as teaching in university settings. Helping other tellers develop stronger skills and deeper artistic lives is my highest accomplishment ... except for raising my children and grandchildren, of course.

AN INTERVIEW WITH ELIZABETH ELLIS

The title of this book says that it is a "storyteller's memoir". When did you become a storyteller?

The truest answer to that question is that I have been a storyteller all my life. I think I came out of the womb telling stories. As a child, I needed to talk as much as I needed to breathe. I got in trouble at school every day. Every single solitary day. Always for the same thing: talking too much. My teachers often said to me, "What on earth will you do when you grow up? All you do is run your mouth." I am grateful that I thought of something.

In 1969 came to Dallas to work for the Dallas Public Library. Storytelling was the part of my job I liked the best. Some days it was the only part I liked. In 1978 I attended the National Storytelling Festival in Jonesborough, Tennessee with my old friend Gayle Ross. We had never heard of anyone making their living as a storyteller. On the long car ride back to Texas, we kept saying, "We could do that. We could do that." About the time we crossed the bridge that spans the Mississippi River, "We could do that." turned into "I'll do it if you will." By the time we got to Dallas the decision was pretty much made that we would quit our regular jobs and become professional storytellers.

Did each of you embark on a solo storytelling career?

No, we began as tandem storytellers, telling together as the Twelve Moon Storytellers. We had heard The Folktellers (Barbara Freeman and Connie Reagan Blake) at the Festival. Their work had a big influence on us. At the time I don't think either of us would have had the nerve to start out on our own. It felt much safer to have a partner when jumping off the cliff, a sort of Butch and Sundance concept, though I wouldn't want to venture which one of us was Butch, and which was Sundance.

How long did you work together?

Four or five years. It was so hard to get work as a storyteller back then it was impossible to make enough money to support our needs. I had kids. Gayle had a horse. They all needed shoes. We needed to go our separate ways in order to pay the bills. Each of us has developed a solo career. Gayle has become a widely respected Cherokee storyteller, focusing most of her energy on sharing Cherokee stories and culture.

Did you hear a lot of stories when you were a child?

Yes, I was lucky enough to have a childhood filled with stories. My grandfather, I. H. Gabbard, was a circuit riding preacher. He might have a dozen or more churches he would travel to in a month's time.

In those days travel was hard in the Appalachian Mountains of Kentucky. He could not go home every night, so he would go home with a family from the church and spend the night with them. That was a pretty standard practice back in those days. That meant he was a guest in many people's homes in the days before radio and television were common. He would listen to the stories at one home and tell them in another home in another community the next night or the following weekend. He did not collect stories like a folklorist would. He recorded them in his head and his heart. When I was a little girl, I thought every one's grandfather knew hundreds of stories.

His daughter, my aunt Ida Gabbard Moore, was an wonderful storyteller, too. She knew and told a lot of the old fairy tales. The stories she told were different from my Grandfather's. She was the most loving person I have ever known.

Have you always been a writer, too?

Yes, I have been fascinated by the concept of writing all my life. As a little girl I was in love with every aspect of it. I mean every aspect of it! When other little girls were playing with their dolls, I was collecting fountain pens and nib pens. I asked for them for Christmases and birthdays.

I made pens out of turkey feathers, too. I did chores for other people to make the money to buy ink. I needed lots of it. But, mostly I made the ink I used. I made it from polk berry juice and walnut hulls and any other plant material I could lay my hands on. As I got older I worked on the colors and the texture, trying to get them just right. Then I discovered the joys of invisible ink. No lemon was ever safe in my presence! I tried to make paper too, but those experiments were always a dismal failure.

I wrote stories throughout my childhood that were "original folktales". As a teenager I graduated to writing teen romance stories. Writing was the private face of storytelling for me. My early experiences with sharing my stories with other people weren't very positive, so mostly I kept them to myself. As I have gotten older I have gotten bolder about sharing what I have written with others, but I still get frightened when doing it.

Are all the stories in this book stories you have told?

I have stories I tell from the stage. I have lots more stories that I tell informally. The "Old Christmas" story is the one I tell informally. Though I have told it many times, I have never shared it from the stage. The others have all been part of public performances.

How does your family feel about being the subject of your stories?

I think of much of my work as being "verbal memoir". I want to tell and write that which will have meaning for other people. Sometimes that requires dipping into subjects that my family members may wish I would keep silent about. Each of them has their own level of need for privacy. I know they have not always been happy with what I have told about them. In some cases it has made them wary of me or driven a wedge between us for a time. It may not seem that way to them, but I work hard to be respectful of their needs. There are lots of stories I choose not to share because of their feelings. There is always the tension between being true to the demands of my art and being true to the needs of my family.

What is the difference between telling a story and setting it down on paper?

When you tell a story you have your tone of voice, your facial expressions and your gestures to help you communicate. When you are writing the same story, you must find a way to do with words all those things that gesture, expression and other non-verbal clues have helped you accomplish. It takes a lot more words on paper to tell the same story you have shared verbally.

One of the major differences is the level of patience that is needed if you are a writer. When you are telling stories, you have listeners right in front of you. You can tell if what you are sharing is being understood. You can see if they are restless or bored. You have the immediate response of laughter, fright or tears. Writing is a solitary pursuit. You probably will never even meet most of your readers. You get no immediate feedback. You have to imagine it for yourself as you go along. Any feedback that comes to you is likely to happen long after the writing process has been completed. So I think writers have to be far more patient people than storytellers are.

Have you published other books?

Yes, I have a book about the crafting of stories titled *From Plot to Narrative*. It was published by Parkhurst Brothers in 2012. I think of it as being a handbook for creating stronger stories of all kinds. Back in 2002, Loren Niemi and I co-authored *Inviting the Wolf In: Thinking About Difficult Stories* (August House). It is about sharing traditional, historical or personal stories that are hard to tell or listen to, those that deal with subjects we find difficult to confront.

Do you have other book projects planned?

I have several ideas for books I would like to do. But, there is no definite plan for what might happen next. We'll have to see what happens.

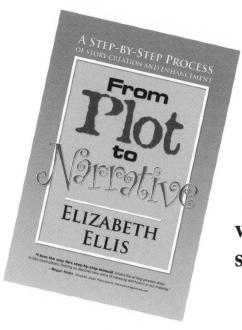

A master storyteller's steps to a better story— for writers and storytellers

"... PLOT IS A WORD EVERYONE HAS HEARD BUT FEW CAN EXPLAIN. It is so much more than "a beginning, a middle, and an end" in a story – as textbooks often define it. Elizabeth Ellis, a master storyteller and teacher, knows better than anyone how to describe the elements of plot and demonstrate how they can be crafted into meaningful stories."
—**Barbara McBride-Smith,** Circle of Excellence Storyteller, School Librarian, and Instructor

"I LOVE THE WAY THIS STEP-BY-STEP MANUAL breaks the writing process down to bite-sized pieces, helping us discover new veins of meaning and humor in our material."
—**Megan Hicks,** Storyteller, Media, Pennsylvania

www.parkhurstbrothers.com